MIRACLES
ARE
FOR REAL

MIRACLES ARE FOR REAL

WHAT HAPPENS WHEN HEAVEN TOUCHES EARTH

JAMES L. GARLOW
AND
KEITH WALL

BETHANY HOUSE PUBLISHERS

a division of Baker Publishing Group
Minneapolis, Minnesota

Published by Bethany House Publishers
11400 Hampshire Avenue South
Bloomington, Minnesota 55438
www.bethanyhouse.com

Bethany House Publishers is a division of
Baker Publishing Group, Grand Rapids, Michigan

Printed in the United States of America

Library of Congress Cataloging-in-Publication Data
Garlow, James L.
    Miracles are for real : what happens when heaven touches earth / James L. Garlow and Keith Wall.
      p. cm.
    Summary: "A comprehensive and straightforward exploration of miracles and divine intervention in both Bible times and the present, written from a Christian perspective"—Provided by publisher.
    ISBN 978-0-7642-0907-9 (pbk. : alk. paper)
    1. Miracles. I. Wall, Keith A. II. Title.
    BT97.3.G37 2011
    231.7'3—dc23   2011029398

Cover design by David Carlson/Studio Gearbox

11 12 13 14 15 16 17   7 6 5 4 3 2 1

I, Jim Garlow, dedicate this book to

CAROL JANE GARLOW

my friend,
my lover,
my advisor,
my "mighty faith person,"
my confidante,
my support system,
my cheerleader,
my spectacular wife of forty years . . .

Who, I pray, regarding her own health,
soon will be able to affirm,

"Miracles are for real!"

I dedicate this book to Ernest Wall,
great father, even greater friend.
Talk about miracles—having you for a dad
counts as one for me.
—Keith

CONTENTS

INTRODUCTION

A MIRACLE AT ANY MOMENT

Whe hen was the last time you hoped for and prayed for a miracle?

A better question: When was the last time you witnessed or even received a miracle in your life?

Frequently we hear the words "What we need is a miracle!" They come from:

- friends and family at the bedside of a sick loved one
- couples huddled over the stack of monthly bills at the kitchen table
- farmers in the grip of a crippling drought
- parents heartsick over their wayward child
- people unemployed and desperate for a paycheck
- spouses clinging to a hope they can keep their marriage together

In fact, we hear pleas for a miracle any time we hope for something marvelous, wondrous, extraordinary, and amazing to happen—something that will meet our deepest needs and desires in an instant of supernatural intervention.

Many are infatuated with the notion that miracles happen, but do most people really believe they do? Or is the idea primarily a relic of a primitive, superstitious past? Do apparent miracles point to a deeper spiritual reality, or are they merely evidence of the human capacity for wishful thinking and self-delusion?

After all, we pride ourselves on being rational people, swayed only by hard evidence and measurable results. By definition, miracles boggle the mind, astound the senses, stagger the imagination, and, yes, defy reason. What place can they possibly have in a society populated by seasoned skeptics and doubters of all things "paranormal"?

In short, are miracles *real*? If the answer is yes, then what do we make of them in today's world?

These are among the questions we'll address as we explore God's powerful and miraculous presence, even in spiritually malnourished times. Along the way, we'll present true-life stories—told accurately and authentically—about people who have experienced miracles.

In Jesus' day, people turned out by the thousands to see and receive miracles of every kind. He healed their diseases, turned water to wine, walked on stormy seas, fed a multitude with little more than a sack lunch—even gave life back to dead people. Who wouldn't drop everything and rush to the countryside to see such things? Who wouldn't believe in miracles afterward? If only we'd been there too!

Well, for anyone yearning to know the truth about miracles, there's good news: Time travel isn't necessary. After examining hundreds of real-life stories told by ordinary people, we've confirmed what we all secretly hope—that life-changing miracles *do* still occur, and with surprising frequency. Inexplicable events that confound logic, and often the very laws of science as we currently understand them, still offer unmistakable evidence of God's daily involvement in our lives.

We have come to believe, and hope you will, too, that miracles are not the "few and far between" phenomena we've taken them to be, reserved for supposed saints and on extraordinary occasions. Miracles just might be more tightly woven into the fabric of our reality than we recognize. C. S. Lewis once said: "Miracles are a retelling in small letters of the very same story written across the whole world in letters too large for some of us to see."[1]

As you read on, we think you'll come to agree with his assessment. Each of the following chapters features a true story of someone who experienced a miracle. In many cases, one of us personally knows the individual being profiled. In other instances, the people were referred to us by someone whose credibility and integrity we trust.

Also included in each chapter is a closer look at some aspect of miracles that sparks interest within nearly everyone's heart, dealing with issues such as whether or not we can persuade God to act, how angels carry out heavenly missions, and why some people experience one miracle or many miracles and others none at all.

Our purposes are simple and straightforward. We want to show that:

God is alive, well, and intensely interested in your life. Some people, especially in times of hardship and heartache, feel that God is a distant observer, nonchalant about the details of our personal daily existence. A close examination of modern-day miracles will prove resoundingly otherwise. Whether you're in need of minor or major intervention, God cares deeply about your needs and circumstances. To put it more directly, God cares deeply about *you*.

Not only do miracles happen, but they still happen today. Throughout recorded history, miracles have taken a place among the most revered accounts and narratives. Some people call these myths, folklore, or legends. To others, miracle stories represent God's mighty handiwork among his creation. We believe the Bible is our true guide for every aspect of life; it's God's message to humankind, and it's our reliable source for wisdom and guidance regarding miracles.

Regarding the supernatural, the best way to live—the only way to live—is to believe that a miracle could happen at any moment. The cliché says, "Hope springs eternal." But this isn't always true. In our most trying times, it's easy to lose hope and give in to despair. The stories and subject matter of this book are intended to show that God is fully capable of doing a great work in your life or the life of someone you love. Every word in the pages to follow affirms and validates what the apostle Paul said: God "is able to do immeasurably more than all we ask or imagine, according to his power that is at work within us."[2] To anyone who has a dreamed-for desire, a desperate plea, or a dire need, these are words to live by.

If it's a miracle you need, and you wonder whether God could do something phenomenal in your life, keep reading, and hold on to those words: *immeasurably more than all we ask or imagine.*

1

DO MIRACLES STILL HAPPEN?

THE VAST MAJORITY BELIEVE

On a cold and snowy Sunday evening in March 1990, Curt Jensen's nerves were frayed before the youth choir road trip he was in charge of even left the parking lot.

Eighty-plus junior high teens from Denver's Rocky Mountain Community Church were finally corralled and loaded into a tour bus and passenger van. It seemed enough luggage to last a year had been stowed. Curt, the youth pastor, made one last head count and one last check to ensure he had everything needed to play ringmaster to this traveling circus over the coming eight days. After months of planning, their concert tour of Idaho at last was set for takeoff.

Curt was accompanied by his pregnant wife, Lori, and a handful of adult chaperones. Among them was Karen Wilson, owner and operator of the sound equipment packed into the caravan's third vehicle, a Chevy Blazer on loan from a congregation member. Her husband, Gil, stayed behind to work, but their two kids—Jackie (eight) and Johnny (six)—had come along for the excursion. Karen volunteered to drive the Blazer so the children could sleep in the backseat through the long night ahead.

The group originally had planned to get underway the following morning but decided to leave early, hoping to cover ground ahead of a winter storm that was forecast to arrive over the next few hours. As the bus driver closed the door and released the air brakes, the first snowflakes were starting to swirl in the headlights. Curt took his seat in the van and sincerely hoped for a little shut-eye sometime before the sun reappeared.

It was a wish that would not come true.

As the convoy headed north on I-25, the van and the Blazer struggled to keep up. Intermittent flurries and gusting winds made driving trickier than usual and put them at a disadvantage compared to the heavy bus and its professional driver. At a fuel stop in Cheyenne, Wyoming, they decided to give up trying to stay together. They'd rendezvous again in a few hours at a landmark truck stop in Evanston, near the Utah border.

Also, Karen reluctantly admitted she was too sleepy to continue driving through the night; Curt agreed to take over while she slept in the bus. One of the chaperones, Dennis, would ride shotgun to keep him company. Jackie and Johnny stayed put in the Blazer, already asleep under blankets.

From Cheyenne, they turned west on I-80 through the rolling short-grass prairie and sagebrush of southern Wyoming.

It was windswept country at the best of times, but past midnight, with the storm gaining strength, it seemed a desolate and empty wilderness. Snowfall increased steadily, and patches of black ice—invisible and treacherous—began to make themselves known without warning on the highway. Driving in the lead, Curt slowed to around forty.

"We'd passed through Laramie and Rawlins with no problems," he said. "Then, about twenty-five miles east of Rock Springs, we came up to a spot where the interstate curved to the right. I turned the wheel and touched the brakes, but the Blazer just kept going straight. We were on black ice, and there was nothing I could do."

As the front driver's-side tire left the pavement, it hit soft snow and dug in, coming to a sudden stop. The Blazer instantly started to roll, carried forward by its momentum. Curt braced against the steering wheel, helpless to do anything but ride it out.

The vehicle flipped three times in a sickening thunder of buckling metal, breaking glass, and the *whump* of equipment crashing around. The Blazer came to rest on its roof. Curt was rattled yet not injured, hanging head-down in his seat belt.

Dennis, momentarily knocked unconscious, quickly came to when Curt called his name. He'd bumped his head and suffered just a bruised shoulder. They could hear Johnny crying in the backseat.

"After seeing we were both okay, I told Dennis we had to get the kids out," Curt recalled. "We opened the doors and got ourselves free. It was pitch black, except for the headlights and the dome light, which struck me as a strange sight, shining up from the ground like that."

They freed Johnny from his seat belt and rapidly checked him over for injuries. Aside from a small forehead cut, he appeared to be unharmed. By this time, the van had come to a safe stop ahead of the scene. Curt passed Johnny to its driver to get him out of the freezing cold.

But it took no time to determine that Jackie was not in her seat. They searched in the back where the speakers and amplifiers lay in a jumble. She wasn't there either. The glass was gone from the window where she'd been resting her head.

"I knew then she must have been thrown from the vehicle, and we started hunting all around in the snow," Curt said. "We couldn't see anything. I couldn't even tell which direction we'd come from. We searched and called her name but found nothing. I was close to losing it, thinking over and over, *What have I done?*"

By then, several passing truck drivers had stopped to help. They brought flashlights and pitched in to comb the ground in every direction. Still, they found no trace of the girl.

Finally, someone suggested the unthinkable—that Jackie might be *under* the Blazer. Curt, Dennis, and six or eight truckers managed to turn it onto its side. Flashlights converged on the sight they dreaded above any other: Jackie lay in the snow, horribly injured. Cuts covered her face and arms, and blood ran from her nose. Her skin was blue, and her head appeared to be crushed. Her disfigured arm obviously was broken.

"She looked dead," Curt remembered. "She wasn't moving or breathing. I'd had CPR training, so without even thinking I dropped beside her to see if I could find a heartbeat. I put my ear to her face and couldn't hear a breath, but I did detect a very faint pulse. I thanked God that at least there was still a chance."

He immediately began administering cardiopulmonary resuscitation, enlisting others to compress Jackie's chest at the appropriate times while he concentrated on breathing for her. After two or three minutes, she coughed, and Curt heard a gurgling sound in her chest when he blew air into her lungs. A trucker produced a piece of heavy cardboard, and they slid her onto it. Another brought blankets to wrap her broken body.

Back at the van, three adults and fourteen teenagers cared for Johnny—and prayed with all their might.

The clock itself seemed to freeze for the next eighty minutes, the time it took for an ambulance to come from Rock Springs. Icy conditions made speed impossible. Curt never left Jackie's side, giving her continuous CPR. Her pulse remained faint, yet she was never able to breathe independently.

"When the ambulance finally arrived, there was a tense moment because it nearly slid off the road itself," Curt recalled. "The crew took over and confirmed she had a slight pulse, but they said it was likely her lungs were collapsed. They checked the rest of us as well; we were fine. They moved her to the ambulance, and I rode with them to the hospital in Rock Springs."

State police gave them an escort; they also issued an alert for officers to locate the bus on the road ahead and inform Lori and Karen about what had happened.

Emergency room doctors confirmed what Curt intuitively had known: Jackie was bleeding internally, her lungs had collapsed, her skull was badly fractured, and her brain was hemorrhaging. She had a broken left arm and multiple cuts and contusions, several of which had required stitches. She still could not breathe on her own.

"It seemed like every fifteen minutes or so they came out and told me more bad news," Curt recalled. "In essence they said she probably wouldn't live. I felt lost, but by this time the van had gotten there, and I remember the waiting room was full of teenagers, all on their knees praying."

Three hours later, the decision was made to airlift Jackie to a children's hospital in Salt Lake City—but the winter storm had grounded all flights for the time being. It took another three hours before they had clearance to go. In the meantime, the authorities had caught up with the tour bus. Officers drove Karen and Lori all the way from Evanston, arriving before the helicopter touched down on the hospital roof.

"After the flight left for Salt Lake, I literally almost gave up," Curt said. "I could barely even pray anymore. I was physically and emotionally exhausted, but there was a totaled vehicle to deal with, and I had to think about what to do with the sound equipment, how to care for the kids from the van, whether to continue on with the trip. To be honest, I wasn't doing well."

He went through the motions; he took the group to breakfast and did his best to comfort and reassure them. Inside, though, he was a tangle of guilt and doubt. How could he have missed the ice on the road? What could he have done differently to keep Jackie safe? Now she'd likely die or, if she survived, she'd be severely challenged for the rest of her life. "Please, God, have mercy" was the only prayer he could utter.

Around one p.m., Curt called Lori from a pay phone, his hands shaking as he dialed the hospital. He was terrified of the news he might hear when his wife finally came to the phone. She answered at last.

Yes, she said, the helicopter had arrived. Yes, she and Karen met the gurney as nurses wheeled it in. No, Jackie actually looked "pretty good"—she'd opened her eyes and said "Mommy" when Karen came to her side. Right, the doctors were shocked, since that's not what they were told to expect, but after re-running all the tests, they couldn't find anything wrong with her.

"What? That *can't* be," Curt stammered. He'd seen Jackie's crushed body with his own eyes, had lifted her from the snow, had kept her alive for more than an hour when she couldn't breathe by herself. He'd seen the looks on the doctors' faces in Rock Springs when they'd told him not to hold out hope. *What do you mean, she's fine?*

"I literally argued with my wife on the phone," he said. "It was very difficult for me to accept. I couldn't be overjoyed at the news. I'd fallen so low I couldn't get back to that place quickly. I just kept thinking, *How?* Of course, I knew there could only be one answer: God had healed her. But I'd seen too much that night to believe it right away."

Five hours later, the crowded van arrived in Salt Lake City. When Curt walked into Jackie's room, she sat up in bed, smiled, and said, "Hi." The disfiguring injuries that had haunted his imagination were gone. Even her cuts and bruises looked minor and well on the way to healing.

"I didn't know what to say," he remembered. "Everyone was acting like it was no big deal, but I said, 'You don't understand!' I just cried. I touched her head and her arm. I asked about her lungs and the bleeding. Absolutely no problems, they said. I got the feeling they thought I'd been exaggerating and that she'd never been as bad off as I said."

What about the X-rays taken in the ER? In fact, doctors in Salt Lake initially were upset with doctors in Rock Springs—for sending the wrong results. Or perhaps they'd sent the wrong girl? All were eventually compelled to admit that somewhere, in the air over southwestern Wyoming, something miraculous had happened.

———

Jackie was released after two days of observation. Karen took her kids home. The concerts proceeded as planned, and the choir performed for packed auditoriums all along the way. Word had spread of Jackie's healing, and everyone wanted to hear the story.

"Many people came to the Lord for the first time that week," Curt said. "But hearing what God had done for Jackie was just as meaningful for those who had been Christians for years. They'd never seen God's power at work so up close and personal."

As the tour caravan passed through Rock Springs on their way back to Colorado the following Saturday, they stopped at a Burger King. Halfway through his meal, Curt noticed an ambulance pull into the parking lot. Several EMTs hurried in and made a beeline for his table. He recognized some from the crew that responded the night of the accident. They'd learned of Jackie's healing and wanted to hear more directly from Curt.

"Tell us everything," they said excitedly.

They listened to his account. They peppered him with questions.

"Do you believe in miracles?" one of the young men asked at last. "Because we sure do now."

A Closer Look

How would *you* answer? If you're like most people, you'd likely say yes, given that 80 percent of Americans believe in miracles. In fact, more people think miracles happen than believe the Bible is God's Word (40 percent) or pray daily (50 percent).[1]

If you don't believe in miracles, perhaps you wish you could. After all, it's a reasonable guess that an interest in miracles is the reason you picked up this book.

But wanting to believe (or even believing) that miracles are possible doesn't mean we don't wrestle with stubborn questions like these . . .

Miracles might be possible, but do they actually still happen?

Is there a God who's involved in the aspects—big and little—of our lives?

Does prayer work?

Can God do a miracle for me?

If I pray for a miracle and it doesn't happen, what does that mean? Does God still love me?

Most people have pondered similar questions at some point. Perhaps you've considered them many times—especially during tough seasons, when you or someone you loved was hurting and needed a change of fortune, if not full-fledged divine intervention.

We want to believe in miracles.

More important, we want to believe they can happen to us and the people we love.

Even so, situations can be hard, circumstances can be painful, and disillusionment is common. Hanging on to what we desire to believe often isn't easy at all.

21

Why We Doubt, Why We Believe

Most of us, at least in some way, at some time, have struggled with believing there's a loving God who's ready and willing to intervene on our behalf. Why do we struggle so? What gets in our way?

Life.

Every day, our faith (in God, miracles, love, hope, you name it) is challenged by things we experience and events we witness. When there's pain or suffering, in our own lives or in the lives of those around us, we may find ourselves questioning and wondering. When there's pain or suffering on a global scale, we're disturbed. When we don't "see" what we interpret as divine intervention, we doubt.

Added to our personal questions are the negative messages we frequently hear from the relative few who decry belief in miracles as something to be dismissed or even scorned. It didn't used to be this way. For centuries, belief in the supernatural wasn't ridiculed but respected. In a different time, many of the greatest scholars also were people of faith who affirmed the miraculous.

Even after this began gradually to change, faith was well represented among those trained and renowned in the sciences. Just three examples:

During the Age of Reason, Blaise Pascal was known for brilliant advancements in math and physics as well as for passionate defense of the Christian faith.

Isaac Newton fervently studied the Bible and described God as "the first cause" that explains how the universe came about.

Juan Lobkowitz, who initially published astronomy tables

when he was ten, became a Cistercian monk and wrote sermons and works of theology.

Not until the late 1800s did a small but vocal minority
cast widespread doubt on belief in the Bible and in miracles
generally. Some of those who contributed to the attack were
biologist Charles Darwin (who recast the creation story to
eliminate God, mystery, and miracle); philosopher Friedrich
Nietzsche (who declared God to be dead); and theologians
Julius Wellhausen and Rudolf Bultmann (who labeled Scripture a myth).

The long shadow of skepticism was cast.

And yet . . .

And yet people still believe. Despite what many scientists
and academicians would tell us, despite constant pain and
suffering all around us, despite our own struggles through
personal wildernesses of doubt and faith, most of us still
believe. In God. In prayer. In heaven touching earth.

Yes, we still believe that God intervenes in our lives in
desperate moments when it seems to matter most. We believe
miracles are for real.

There's no question about it: Jackie's healing was a miracle.
There's also no question that our minds struggle to grasp the
impossibility of her almost-immediate restoration to health
even as our spirits soar at the thought.

Obviously, a crushed body made inexplicably whole during a brief "flight for life" is supernatural. Are there also
other kinds of divine intervention? Can a "coincidence" be a
miracle? Is fortuitous timing a miracle? What about a much-
needed change, preceded by great effort and hard work—can't
that be a miracle too?

Jackie's story is truly amazing, and in the coming pages

we'll share more that will leave you encouraged and in awe. But first, a few things to know about miracles.

What Kind of Miracle Are You Seeking?

Jesus performed miracles in five different arenas common to humanity.

He intervened in the human *heart*, which we call salvation.

He intervened in the human *body*, which we call healing.

He intervened in human *emotions*, which we call deliverance.

He intervened in *nature*, such as when he calmed the storm.

He intervened in *death* by raising people from the dead.

If you're in need of a touch from heaven, what are you longing for? Do you or someone you love need a miracle of the heart? The body? The emotions? Do you need something in your world to change? Do you need victory in some area?

Finally, are you longing for a work of creation or of providence?

Miracles of creation supersede nature's basic known laws. We see creative miracles throughout the Bible, such as when Jesus multiplied five fish and two loaves of bread into enough food to feed five thousand men plus women and children. Or when God created the energy to divide the Red Sea. Or when Jesus made blind eyes see, or turned water into wine.

As for miracles of provision, *providence* refers to God's intervention at a critical moment. That is, these are miracles of timing, also found throughout Scripture.

Sometimes Jesus accelerated an event so that it happened sooner or delayed an event so that it took place later than it normally would have. Sometimes he made things happen precisely when he dictated rather than letting them take their natural course.

The fig tree withering and dying before its time was a providential miracle. Jericho's walls collapsing exactly when the Israelites blew their trumpets was providential. Demons being cast out of people "ahead of schedule"—also providential.[2]

You've picked up this book for a reason. Whatever it is, we invite you to open your heart and mind to the people and stories in its pages. If you have personal doubts or unanswered questions, read on. Inspiration and answers lie just ahead.

Despite tough times, despite pain and suffering—even despite our seasons of disillusionment or doubt—miracles really do happen. Can they happen in your life?

Let's find out.

2

GOD MOVES IN MANY MYSTERIOUS WAYS

EXPLORING THE LEVELS OF DIVINE INTERVENTION

If you need a miracle in your life, you're not alone. Far from it.

Maybe you're reading this book out of intellectual or theological curiosity. It's a fascinating topic, and who doesn't want fresh insights to ponder and captivating stories to consider?

It's likelier you have a more personal motivation—you're waiting, hoping, praying for God to reveal himself and intercede in a powerful way.

You may feel isolation in your desire or desperation for a miraculous act in your life. But, once again, you can be re-assured you're on a shared journey of longing and expectation. Fellow travelers are walking alongside.

Jim's Journey: "We Need a Miracle"

This book is a joint effort of two writers, so most often we use the collective "we" to refer to us, the coauthors. For the next few pages, though, please allow me, Jim, to share part of my story that's highly personal. I want to discuss a topic about miracles—at least about the need for one—that's tender and delicate to my family and me.

Just this morning, I sat with my wife, Carol, in the office of her oncologist. The discussion centered upon her four-year battle with a rare form of cancer called primary peritoneal carcinoma. So far, the path has consisted of a first diagnosis followed by two remissions and two disappointing recurrences. As we considered in serious tones the latest test results, I referred to "that phone call." The specialist knew which one I meant.

On only a single previous occasion had I referred to *that call:* when my wife was away from home, and it was just the doctor and me on the phone. I asked the question no caregiver wants to ask: "Barring a miracle—which we're truly counting on—how long does she have?"

I could barely believe those words were coming from my mouth. He responded straightforwardly, with a time frame that literally sent a shiver convulsing through my body. I hope you'll understand my choice not to share that response right now, since it's highly sensitive and private to us.

That call occurred a few months ago. And there we were today, back in his office, going over more results yet again. Carol's chemotherapy, the third extensive round in three years, was coming to an end. The cancer markers weren't nearly as good as we'd expected. Our conversation turned to the contents of "that phone call" and the prognosis.

He explained something we already knew: Carol was "outside medical literature," so he had little to go on. He couldn't prognosticate what might happen to one person; he could outline the "average" of what would happen to a hundred patients. Starting with the most difficult news, he stated that some would have only a few months to live. Others would live much longer. So the best he could do was take the average life expectancy among all those studied and base his "best estimate" on that.

And then he said something that was music to our ears: "Some people would continue to live a long time, and there would simply be no medical explanation for it. They would be living a miracle."

Although Carol's oncologist and I have deep love and respect for each other—and I would truly call him a friend—I suspect he wouldn't necessarily share my particular spiritual convictions.

But his words stirred a strong sense of hope in us. Not false expectation or wishful thinking. *Strong hope*. It's a needed ally for those in daunting and disheartening circumstances.

This whole idea isn't an academic exercise or a theoretical concept for me. It's a real-world, day-and-night, life-or-death issue. As I write, my wife needs a miracle. And she needs it soon. Few survive five years after the first diagnosis, and we're at the four-year marker. Having gone from Stage IIIc to Stage IV doesn't help the situation.

We have hope and faith, though—lots of both. We're not in denial. We know what we face, yet this does not keep us from expecting to beat the odds with a genuine God-sent miracle.

Thus when I'm seeking to respond to the question "Do miracles exist today?" it's a very personal, enormously important, and extremely emotional matter to me and my wife. This is no intriguing abstraction to muse upon while puffing on a pipe and stroking my chin in an ivory tower. I'm right there in the trenches, struggling and searching.

Attempting to Define *Miracle*

That interaction with the oncologist raised an important question. The definition of a miracle the doctor used essentially was "an occurrence that cannot be explained by our current understanding of medical science." Another version goes like this: "An event that appears inexplicable by the laws of nature and so is held to be supernatural in origin or an act of God."

Those are helpful blanket definitions, and we'll talk more about that in the next chapter. For now, understand this: *Not all miracles are created equal.* That is, there are different categories, or levels, of divine intervention.

For example, something that defies all possible odds could also be a miracle. Suppose a single parent needs exactly $2,361.48 by Friday to pay two months' rent or she and her three kids will be evicted. Despite her growing panic, she tells no one of the need—except God, in fervent prayer. No human except her landlord could possibly know that exact amount, yet an out-of-state check for $2,361.48 from someone she knew many years ago arrives in Thursday's mail.

Did that actually defy science? Technically, no. Yet the odds of it happening are so remote that this likely would qualify. Thus, while a miracle might not necessarily be inexplicable scientifically, it might defy all probability nevertheless.

A more challenging test regarding a miracle's definition involves answers to prayer. Envision yourself in an emergency situation, far removed from any aid. You place call after call on your cell phone, to no avail. You're out of coverage range. There hasn't for a moment been a single bar on the screen— and no help is coming.

In desperation, you fall to your knees and cry out to God, asking for the phone to work. Finishing your pleas, you dial one more time. Suddenly, for reasons unexplainable, you're connected with 9-1-1. Help is on the way.

Was that a miracle? To the one in acute need, it sure felt like one. But maybe, maybe not.

It's possible that there's a distinction between profound answers to prayer and miracles. While some of the stories in this book will involve an amazing and inexplicable reply to a prayer, for the most part we've tried to stick with that which defied known science.

What about coincidences? As many have said, in various words, "The more I pray, the more coincidences I have!" They mean that prayer produces results. And it does.

While it's not necessarily the same as a miracle, an answer to prayer still is a wondrous event, something to cherish and celebrate. Any activity of God in our lives even further demonstrates his already extensively evidenced love for us. Attaching a classification other than *miracle* makes it no less fantastic.

Even so, how then do we attempt to classify or categorize various acts of God? Well, one way to approach this is to proffer a sort of "scale of the inexplicable," from great to greater to greatest (graded one to five).

(1) The Simplest Answered Prayer

Imagine a little girl whose beloved dog has wandered away. She's distraught, knowing he's been gone three days; family search-and-rescue efforts have come up empty. She prays, asking God to please bring her puppy home. Minutes later, she hears a bark in the front yard. He's found his way back!

Was that a miracle? Likely not. But it was a meaningful and personal answer to prayer.

(2) The Complex Answered Prayer

This is a remarkable answer that extends well above the dog-come-home example. Suppose two parents are distraught about their seventeen-year-old son, whose experimentation with drugs has led him into methamphetamine addiction. Despite loving offers to help him overcome his problem, they discover one evening that he's packed a bag and disappeared. Desperate days turn into weeks as they anxiously fear for his life. They mobilize fellow church members and a network of friends and family to pray by name for their son's safe return.

After five silent weeks, he's discovered at a rescue mission—several hundred miles away. The volunteer who found him and arranged for his return was a friend of someone in the parents' congregation. He didn't know their family but recognized the name from the prayer request forwarded via email.

Was it a miracle, or did this guy "just happen" to recognize the teenager's name? We don't know, but to those heartsick parents, it's a complex answer to prayer: God intervened to bring those circumstances together for good.

(3) The "Coincidence"

This is a set of circumstances that doesn't necessarily involve specific prayer but still produces amazing results. Imagine you've been unemployed for nearly a year. Your life has been a gradual slide downward. Your savings account has dwindled to zero, and your house may be repossessed. Even buying groceries has become a weekly test of faith. All this despite the dozens of applications and résumés you've submitted, along with a few actual interviews. It all seemingly has come to naught.

Until, that is, you get an out-of-the-blue call. "I got your name from a trusted source," the voice on the line says. "I think you might have the skills and experience we're seeking. Business is booming, and we're staffing up. How soon can you come in for a meeting?"

You're stunned—and extremely grateful. How did she find you? She explains that her sister overheard you telling your plight to someone at your kid's Little League game. The sister knew of you, inquired about your credentials, and passed your name along. After all the months of fruitless efforts, this connection came together so quickly and easily. And "coincidentally."

(4) "Against All Odds"

This is an event that utterly defies probability: something anyone would say has no actual or reasonable chance whatsoever of happening. Let's say twins, a boy and a girl, were

33

given up for adoption as infants. In their teen years, they both learned they had a sibling "out there somewhere" yet had no way of tracking each other down. They've lived their entire lives two thousand miles apart. For many years, these two people longed to meet and get acquainted.

Then, when they're thirty-five, they each choose a vacation in Hawaii. At a resort mixer, they're seated next to each other and strike up a conversation. One thing leads to another, and another, and another. Before long, the two are hugging tightly, tears streaming down both faces. Astoundingly—against all odds—the long-lost, separated-at-birth twins were reunited, only because several extraordinary synchronicities brought them together.

(5) A Miracle

This is an event that extends beyond all known scientific laws. There are many such stories in this very book—astonishing, mind-boggling accounts that leave us saying, "How could that happen? It *had* to be God!"

We're in no way denigrating or dismissing any of the other "levels." In fact, we rejoice over them. Again, even an answer to the simplest prayer is an act of divine intervention. That's part of the adventure and the ongoing excitement for people of faith: We never know how or when God's going to show up.

Although we're attempting to categorize different phenomena, who really can say what is or isn't *miraculous?* God truly does move in mysterious—and in many different—ways.

The following story is a good test case for deciphering and discerning the supernatural phenomena "pecking order." To

34

us, the extraordinary experiences of Ron and Dianne Earl fall firmly into the miracle category. But see what you think.

"His Family Still Needs Him!"

Ron Earl got out of bed early on June 9, 1990. While heavy overnight rainfall had mellowed into intermittent showers, the summer sky was still overcast and dark. He tiptoed through the house as he dressed, careful not to wake his family.

It was Saturday, but Ron had a midmorning meeting scheduled in Columbus, Ohio, which was a two-and-a-half-hour drive from his home in Toledo, at the western tip of Lake Erie. He and two bank colleagues—Steve Jones and Bob Dittman—met for breakfast at 5:30, then an hour later were headed south on Interstate 75 in Steve's Pontiac Cutlass. Bob sat in the back, while Ron had hopped into the front passenger seat.

"There was water everywhere," Ron recalled. "I didn't realize just how much it had rained already, till we got going. There were lakes standing in the fields and on the roadsides. Still, everything was great. We were laughing and having a good time."

Rain continued to fall now and again. Near Columbus, Highway 23 widened to four total lanes, with a shared turn lane in the middle. Steve kept to the left, in the lane nearest the center, to avoid the standing pools at the edges. He kept their speed around forty-five.

Another driver approached from the rear and decided to pass them on the right. She wasn't traveling excessively fast, but it was enough to cause her car to hydroplane on a sheet of water. She lost control and began to drift into the left lane.

To avoid certain contact, Steve veered toward the highway's center.

"I have no memory of what happened next," Ron said. "The only way I know anything at all is from reading the police reports."

The Cutlass was struck first by an oncoming car in the turn lane. This glancing collision spun them into northbound traffic. By the time they came to a stop, they had been hit by five other vehicles, with devastating force.

Steve Jones died instantly. Bob Dittman survived but with life-altering back injuries.

Rescuers had to use the Jaws of Life to cut open the wreckage and extract the unconscious and badly broken Ron Earl.

———— ⌖ ————

The sun had finally emerged in Toledo. Dianne Earl fed the children breakfast and then sent them off to play at a neighbor's house.

"It was beautiful after all that rain," she remembered. "When I got the call from the hospital in Columbus, it was hard to even comprehend what I was hearing. Once it sank in, my only thought was to pray harder than I'd ever prayed. I ran down the sidewalk to get the kids and bring them home."

A handyman was working downstairs, so Dianne took the children—ages ten, seven, and four—upstairs to her son's bedroom. She gathered them in her arms and told them what had happened. Then she prayed.

"I cried out to God like never before," Dianne said. "At this point I still didn't know how bad Ron's condition was, but I said, 'Dear God, we still need him! His family still needs him!'"

She began making calls, and gradually word spread to friends and family. The phone started ringing with offers of help. Dianne's mother arrived to watch the kids while her father drove her to Columbus.

———— ∞∞∞ ————

When Ron "woke up," he was standing in a place like nowhere and nothing he'd ever seen—a featureless white room filled with a pleasantly bright light. He was not alone; Steve Jones stood at his side, apparently unharmed. They looked at each other in surprise and with mild confusion. Neither spoke, but each understood the question on the other's mind: *Where are we?* Quickly it dawned on them that they were dead.

At that moment, Ron felt someone lightly touch his shoulder. He turned in time to see a man in a flowing white robe disappear through a doorway at the top of a short stairway.

"I can't explain how, but I knew immediately that this was Jesus and that he had brought us here," Ron said. "We knew we'd been killed and that we were in heaven. I felt the most incredible peace, like I didn't have a single care in the world. None of the things we normally worry about seemed to matter at all."

Then, without leaving the room, Ron saw Dianne and his kids walking together, toward home, along their neighborhood sidewalk. It was as if a window had opened in the floor and he could watch them from above. He realized Dianne must have heard about the accident by now, but he felt none of the fear and anguish he normally would have experienced at the thought of what they must be enduring. Ron simply "knew" that everything would be all right and that God would take care of his family. He felt as "lighthearted as a child, excited and happy."

Then a male voice spoke, soothingly and compassionately but also resounding with power and authority: "You need to go back. Your family still needs you."

Ron recalled: "I always expected God's voice to be loud and booming, but it was so natural, just like when people speak to each other. There was no debating what he said, though, that's for sure. I was going to go back because he's in charge. It was such a comforting feeling, like when you're a scared little kid, but then your dad picks you up and you aren't scared anymore. I was thirty-six at the time, and I felt like I was being tucked into bed again."

He looked at Steve and motioned for him to come along, but his friend shook his head. Realizing he was to return alone, Ron turned toward a dark place that had appeared in the wall. He took one step forward and instantly was back in his body, strapped to an operating table.

Unable to move, he looked around the ER. Numerous X-rays hung along the walls, and at least a dozen doctors stood talking together, paying him no attention. Aside from their conversation, the room was eerily quiet. Ron caught on that the physicians were trying to decide what to list as his cause of death.

The neurosurgeon said, "I'm not sure why his brain flatlined, because when we looked at it, we couldn't find anything."

"And that struck me as really amusing," Ron recalled, "because whenever I'd get into trouble as a kid my mother would say, 'You must not have anything in that brain of yours.'"

So he spoke up clearly: "Funny—that's just what my mom used to say!"

All the personnel spun around on the spot and stared at Ron in shock. Instantly the monitors started beeping again.

The surgical teams leapt into action. The lead surgeon rushed to Ron's side and began firing questions: "What's your name? Remember what day it is? Can you move your toes?" He listed the injuries indicated by X-rays and CT scans: severe head trauma; broken shoulder, neck, collarbone, back, and pelvis; shattered right knee; massive internal bleeding. Ron's brain had stopped, also, before they could decide what to repair first. For nearly twenty minutes he'd shown no sign of life.

"He started to tell me what surgeries they needed to perform now that I'd regained consciousness, but it puzzled him that my blood pressure was suddenly normal," Ron said. "So he ordered another round of tests."

This time the results were dramatically different: no evidence of internal bleeding; no head injury; his knee, though still painful and swollen "like a basketball," had been put back together; all broken bones except his collarbone were mended. The staff continued running diagnostics through the afternoon, trying to fathom what had just happened.

"It was beyond their experience," he said. "The chief surgeon still wanted to do exploratory surgery—to see it with his own eyes, I suppose. They never did offer me an official explanation, but a lot of the nurses kept coming around, wanting to hear what had happened."

Ron went from being listed in "critical condition" to "serious" to "fair" in a single day. He went home Monday, less than forty-eight hours after the crash that had killed his friend and left the car without "a single straight piece of metal anywhere on it."

His body was covered in deep purple bruises; his knee was sore and swollen. His collarbone was broken. Bits of glass from the shattered windshield were imbedded in his arm.

Yet he was alive.

"To this day I have a bump on my collarbone," Ron said. "I think God gave me that as a reminder of what he can do and how close his miraculous help really is."

———⟨∞⟩———

Ron didn't tell anyone right away about his heavenly experience, for fear of being called crazy. But two weeks later, Dianne finally shared how she'd gone to get their children and how they had passionately prayed together: *His family still needs him!*

"I told her I'd seen her and the kids on the sidewalk and what God had said to me. We looked at each other in amazement when it hit us that her prayer was exactly the phrase God used: 'Your family still needs you.'"

People often ask if Ron wishes he hadn't come back. It's a tough call, he says, since heaven is "a great place where we have no worries at all." Then he thinks of his fourth child, Laura, born four years afterward, and of all the opportunities he has now to live for God and his family.

Reflecting on his extraordinary experience, Ron says, "I came back with the feeling that I didn't want to just go through the motions of my life anymore. I wanted to do exactly what God wants, and not just coast along. I worry a lot less now. I get concerned from time to time, like we all do while still on this side of heaven. But it's easier for me to know that God is in control. Most of all, I don't fear death anymore. When my time comes, I know what to expect."

3

THE REAL DEAL

WHAT CONSTITUTES AN ACTUAL MIRACLE?

You may have noticed that the word *miracle* is thrown around a lot these days. Miracle-Gro helps plants thrive. Miracle Whip is slathered on sandwiches. A Miraclesuit is swimwear that promises to help women look ten pounds lighter in ten seconds. We hear of miracle supplements, miracle drugs, and miracle cures.

The 1980 U.S. Olympic hockey team's improbable upset of the Russians was dubbed "The Miracle on Ice." (Cue the famous recording of Al Michaels gushing, "Do you believe in miracles? *Yes!*") In 2009, when the extraordinary Captain Chesley "Sully" Sullenberger landed a plane full of people on a river near Manhattan, news media called it "Miracle on the Hudson."

Can every impressive event or product be considered miraculous? Of course, most often the term is used colloquially—to get attention or to stick in minds. But it's worth asking: What really is a miracle? How can we define an act of divine intervention versus occurrences that are merely coincidental or good luck?

Miracles: Fact or Fiction?

Lots of people grow up hearing about miracle stories in Sunday school, bedtime books, or movies. They learn about Daniel in the lion's den, the parting of the Red Sea, Jonah being swallowed up and spit out by a great fish, and Noah keeping animals safe and dry amid the worldwide flood. Then there are accounts of Jesus walking on water, causing the blind to see, and raising people from the dead. What wonderful stories!

But are they just stories?

For some people, outgrowing the innocence and wonder of childhood means becoming a skeptical and "rational-thinking" adult. All those biblical stories that fired their imagination and fueled their curiosity as kids seem, from an adult perspective, outlandish and unbelievable. They may say, "The dramatic events in the Bible, and the big God in the sky who caused them, are good grist for novels and movies. But they probably have nothing to do with the real world."

Does this type of thinking sound familiar? If asked, most people would confess belief in some kind of deity. But when pressed about whether this same God performs contemporary miracles, like those we read about in the Bible, many respond with understandable skepticism.

Few subjects lend themselves to so much confusion and misunderstanding as does "the matter of miracles." Many who accept the existence or possibility of miraculous events go through life without expecting to witness amazing phenomena such as recorded by the apostles and prophets in Scripture. Christians and other theists (believers in God) often point out that miracle accounts are a secondary biblical theme, the primary theme being God's love and salvation.

It's true that God is far more interested in *relating* to you than amazing you with special effects and supernatural acts. Still, if every narrative of the miraculous were removed from the Bible, there would be a *substantial* amount redacted. Besides, if disbelief in miracles causes one to reject the entire Bible, then God's main message—of love and mercy—also is lost. Thus, a thorough discussion of miracles is unavoidable for anyone who takes issues of faith seriously.

A Matter of Perspective

Perhaps you've heard a doubting person ask something like this: "If those miracle stories are true, then why don't we see similar things happening today? If the same God is around and even watches over us now, shouldn't he be doing the same stuff he supposedly did thousands of years ago?"

The short answer to this fair question is, "God does indeed continue to do miracles." One who affirms and anticipates modern-day miracles, however, likewise must understand the purpose behind ancient miracles, especially if we agree that they come and always have come from the same source: a God who hasn't changed and won't change.

In any discussion, it's helpful if initially we agree on the essential or basic parameters of what we're considering. Specifically, the word *miracle* far too often pops up without a suitable definition. For our purposes, let's say that a miracle is "a phenomenon performed or prompted by God, which science cannot explain, at a special time when God is making his will or his love known to an individual or many individuals."

You'll notice there's nothing "anti-science" about our denotation. We're talking about something science cannot *currently* explain or clarify. Often, in debates between atheists and theists, the issue of science *versus* Scripture comes up. Belief in natural evidence and belief in supernatural phenomena are viewed as oppositional, as gloved foes throwing punches. That's unfortunate.

When the Bible speaks of miracles, we're not meant to assume that God waved his hands like a magician and completely disregarded natural law. God, as Creator of the universe, also is the Creator of what we understand to be these very principles (the laws of nature). Therefore, an open mind ought not presume that miracles are out of the question.

If science has taught us one lesson over the ages, it's that humankind frequently learns to do things previous generations would have thought (or actually did think) impossible.

For millennia it was believed that the sun revolved around the earth—until Galileo cogently demonstrated otherwise.

Early-twentieth-century textbooks insisted that the atom could never be split. Before long, textbooks had to be revised.

Imagine somebody in 900 BC seeing a Ferrari or a 3D LCD display. Or imagine him merely seeing a Model-T or a silent film! Through his eyes, such technology would appear astonishing and inexplicable. To us, these aren't miracles but rather a harnessing of scientific law that those who came before us had not yet discovered.

With this in mind, it's easy to suggest that humans a thousand years from now will be able to do things beyond what we even can hypothetically posit or envision today. If it's so straightforward to count on our descendants for amazing future accomplishments and feats, why is it so difficult to accept that God could arrange and orchestrate such phenomena here and now?

The key to understanding the word *miracle* is in first defining another word: *science*.

How do *you* define science? Your mind might meander back to high school biology, where the smell of formaldehyde oozed from dismembered frogs in a room wallpapered with periodic tables. That's a great beginning. Science, you learned, is the study of observable laws.

In that class, and in others, you also learned that the world and the world beyond our world function in certain predictable ways. Again, we call these laws *scientific* laws.

But what if something happens that's outside or beyond these known laws? What if things happen that appear to defy or violate them? We tend to identify that as a miracle. However, as we've stated elsewhere, a miracle isn't necessarily something that violates a scientific law; it merely supersedes a known law. It's beyond what we presently understand.

Could this mean, then, that a miracle can happen without God? If, say, we only know 1 percent of what there is to know, with 99 percent of scientific laws yet to be discovered, then who needs God for a miracle, right? Couldn't a miracle just be the laws of science—unknown by us to this point—at work without involvement from God?

Not exactly. The thing that makes a miracle a miracle is

either God's capacity for miraculous timing or God's capacity to create.

Once more, God's doing of a miracle generally involves one of two inexplicable things:

- *The telescoping or expansion of massive amounts of time.* For instance, if someone is healed instantly, it could be that what would have taken a year happened in a second. If a person comes back to life, is it possible that time was turned backward for her? Since God is God, he can do these types of things.

- *The creation of something.* The Creator of heaven and earth has the power and ability to create in miraculous fashion. Consider the creation of matter (Jesus feeding five thousand men and their families with a few fish and bread loaves); the creation of energy, force, or power (parting the sea); the creation of order, information, or complexity (healing two blind men at Jericho, turning water into wine); the creation of biological life (raising Lazarus); the creation of spiritual life, or spiritual renewal (conversion of Saul, later called Paul).

"Science talk" can get incredibly complex, and many volumes have been written trying to explain the connection between the natural and the supernatural. For our purposes, it's important to know that God does flow within the true laws of science, as he created them. While human understanding changes with each generation, truth—all of which is God's—is unchanging.

The other important point: God is intricately involved in his creation, highly involved in our world (and the worlds beyond). We label his interaction with this world—what we do not grasp—as "miraculous."

A Theological Trick Question

People dubious about supernatural activity sometimes like to trot out a well-worn trick in the skeptic's playbook. They ask: "If God can do anything, can he create a rock so big that even he won't be able to move it?"

This question may sound as old as God himself. Theologians and scholars have heard it as often as cynics have thought of it. Many doubters bring it up with humility and sincerity, seeking an honest answer. Others do so condescendingly, believing they're clever and expecting Christians to fall out of their chairs.

The answer surprises many. *It's false to say that God can do anything* (meaning "everything," as in, "there's nothing God cannot do"). If that stopped you in your tracks, hold on.

Scripture proclaims God's astonishing attributes and abilities, which are inexpressibly above and beyond ours. The ancient Hebrews spoke often and rightly of God's *omnipotence,* or "all-powerfulness." Sometimes they did so hyperbolically, in the sense of expressing that, in so many words, "God can do anything."

When the biblical writers tell us God can do anything, they mean "anything that's possible to do." We say this includes miracles, because while such wondrous works may be beyond our limited understanding, God knows things—truth—that we don't yet comprehend. God can perform miracles *because it is possible to do miracles.*

However, some things are, literally, impossible.

For instance, Scripture goes out of its way to show that God can never be evil. That a good God cannot be an evil God is rather obvious, but even if we wanted to set aside moral and ethical considerations, neither could such a supposition hold up under the scrutiny of logic.

The same holds true for the omnipotent God/immovable rock concept. It posits a God who can do anything but then rearranges matters so that he *cannot* do something. No such "rock" could be created—in fact, nothing can be "created" that is greater than its uncreated Creator. The notion itself is senseless.

A truly open mind won't assume that miracles are impossible; the history of science has provided evidence to the contrary. After all, the term *miracle* is merely a descriptive word for something science currently cannot explain. Our opinion is that human beings probably know less than 1 percent of all available knowledge. How, then, does God do miracles? Within the 99 percent we *don't* yet have. The idea is not to throw science or critical thought out the window. If we embrace humility and keep an open mind in considering the miraculous, we're poised to receive a Creator who loves us and wants us to know him.

There's another essential facet to this: A miracle happens "at a special time when God is making his will or his love known to an individual or many individuals." God doesn't need to flex his muscles and show off to impress us. When he intervenes, he does so to demonstrate his care for us.

With this in mind, read the following true account of how God performed a miracle—acted in a way that's unexplainable by current scientific knowledge—and displayed his love through a most unlikely person.

Modern-Day Miracle: Wonder Woman

On a Friday morning in early November 2006, the sun rose in a cloudless sky. Lydia Collins marveled that though the year's first winter storm was due to arrive by nightfall, she wouldn't have known it by observing people on the streets of her Colorado hometown.

The autumn had been mild, and the day's pleasant temperature was a blessing the residents of this mountain town did not take for granted. When winter finally came, they knew five long months lay ahead before it again departed. One more day of shorts and T-shirts might be all they had left for a while—and they intended to enjoy it.

Lydia was less cavalier about the coming seasonal change, for a personal reason. She'd agreed to pick up Nolan, her six-year-old grandson, after school and take him to the dentist so her daughter and son-in-law wouldn't need to miss work. She was happy to help out, and at any rate the possibility of slick streets wasn't what concerned her. On her mind was the fifteen-mile uphill trip to take Nolan back home to his family's cabin. If the storm struck as expected, they could run into snow and ice on the remote winding roads, a series of switchbacks that could seem treacherous even in the best of conditions.

Sure enough, by midafternoon Lydia knew that the weatherman had gotten the forecast right. The approaching squall had already tossed a dense blanket of gray over the formerly sunny sky. She decided that if it started to snow by the end of Nolan's appointment, she'd call her daughter and insist he stay overnight with her in town.

The thought eased her mind as she pulled her trusty Subaru out of the garage and headed out. Why take the risk of being caught in a blizzard when she could share a safe and cozy evening with her grandson? They would play board games and drink hot chocolate. Getting him to school in the morning would be far easier and more sensible than braving twisty, maybe icy, mountain roads.

"I'm not a terribly adventurous person," she recalled later. "I was relieved to have a plan that didn't involve any heroics."

However, that's not what God had in mind. As she sat in the dentist's waiting room, flipping idly through magazines, Lydia began to have second thoughts. Without understanding why, she suddenly felt it was important for Nolan to be in his own home that night. She battled internally for forty-five minutes, her resolve swinging one way and then the other. She wanted to rely on pure prudence and make a commonsense decision, but she couldn't deny that intuition said keeping her grandson in town tonight would be a mistake. There was a *reason,* she felt, even if she didn't know what it was.

By the time Nolan emerged with freshly cleaned teeth, Lydia had resigned herself to making the trip. She'd lived long enough to recognize one of God's nudges—and knew better than to ignore it. *At least it hasn't begun to snow,* she thought, as they climbed in the car and buckled up.

The roads weren't dry for long. As soon as they crossed the city limits, a light drizzle began to fall. The moisture made the last colorful leaves look shiny and vivid even in the muted light, as if they were covered in wet shellac. Then the wind came up and soon was thrashing the tops of the towering pines lining the road.

Lydia's confidence started to shrivel. There was no denying it: The storm was upon them. Still, she drove on, determining not to third-guess herself and instead to trust the choice God had led her to.

As she rounded a slow curve, she was keenly watching for the turn she would make to reach her daughter's house. Even so, she nearly didn't see the man lying under his big vehicle on the shoulder, his legs stretched out perilously onto the road. Instinctively she tapped the brakes and pulled off behind the truck, which was loaded to capacity with cut firewood.

The man was just behind the dual rear wheels on the driver's side. Lydia looked at her cell phone and wasn't surprised when the display indicated no available service—there rarely was in these tight mountain canyons.

"Stay in the car," she told Nolan. "I'm going to see if he needs anything."

The boy's eyes were wide as he watched from the backseat. He hadn't expected to see his petite and proper grandmother march into a storm to aid a person who looked to have been covered with grease and dirt *before* he climbed under his truck.

The drizzle was turning to snow.

Lydia approached and saw that the man was struggling with a set of snow chains. If his destination lay on the other side of the upcoming mountain pass, he wouldn't think of attempting it in this weather without the extra traction. But the chains appeared to be caught on something as he strained to pull them free. Growling and swearing, he clearly was unaware of Lydia's arrival.

"Want me to call for help?" she offered, feeling tentative but speaking loudly because of the wind.

The man grew still and stopped cursing at the sound of her voice. He was in his early thirties, she guessed, with dark hair and a grizzled beard.

"I can't get reception here," she continued, "but I could call when I get where we're going. It's not very far away."

He looked at her from under the truck, embarrassed that somehow he'd been overheard even above this racket by such a dainty old lady. "No, gonna get this thing un*stuck*!" he yelled. "It's just wedged in there."

He went back to work on an incomprehensible tangle of chain and wire and bungee cord hanging from the undercarriage.

"Well, one reason I stopped is to say you're partly in the road." She felt she was almost shouting. "You could be run over!"

Without reply, he shifted himself to move slightly off the pavement.

As he did, Lydia thought the truck edged backward slightly—almost imperceptibly. This stretch of road had no flat ground; he'd stopped on a steep incline, facing uphill. In the fading light, Lydia couldn't be sure she could trust her eyes, but tingles quickly ran up her spine, and all her senses were on high alert.

Not wanting to tell the man his business, she decided to ask anyway: "Sir, are you sure the parking brake is set well?" She was now acutely aware that the stranger under the wheels wasn't the only one in danger: Nolan, in her car, was directly behind the truck. If the brakes gave way, she would not have time to move the car or get him out.

"I'm sure," he growled. "Think I'd be under here if I wasn't?"

"Well, I think I saw everything move backward a little. Maybe you could come out here and—"

Just then the emergency brake cable groaned under the strain. The truck began to move.

The man hollered an expletive and began scrambling to get out of the wheels' path.

Lydia was momentarily frozen in place, unable to decide whether to help him to safety or run for Nolan, who was unaware of the danger.

"I'm caught!" the man howled. "My jacket is caught!"

The brakes were beginning to fail completely. The man thrashed to stay ahead of the rolling wheels, a race he was losing, at imminent risk of being crushed against the ground.

Without hesitation, Lydia sprang forward and put her hands and shoulder against the corner of the tailgate. With all her might she leaned into the weight of the truck. She kept fighting, didn't give up . . . and the whole thing came to a stop.

The heavy vehicle—and its massive load—*reversed* course and moved uphill several feet, giving the man time and slack to get free. He jumped to his feet, hurried to the cab, and pulled the brake lever upward a few inches so it was fully engaged and able to hold the weight.

Lydia let go. She felt winded but otherwise unharmed.

The man walked back to where she stood. They looked at each other for several long moments, stunned and speechless.

"What just happened?" he said, trembling with adrenaline and shock. "Are you okay?"

Still overwhelmed by what had transpired in a matter of seconds, Lydia shook her head and heaved a sigh. "I'm fine. I think God just did a miracle."

The man let out a hoot, brushing back his wet hair with shaking hands. "I think you should get the credit. You're the one who did the Wonder Woman act."

"Trust me, I'm no hero," she said. "That was God."

The fellow swung his head back and forth, trying to take it all in. "Well, between the two of you, you saved my skin."

And possibly Nolan's too, Lydia thought. *Now I know why we were supposed to make this trip.*

The rest of the trek was uneventful. Nolan and Lydia made it home safe and sound. She and the man whose life she likely saved exchanged phone numbers and became acquainted. Although not a man of faith, he visited Lydia's church on occasion, impressed and intrigued by the "spiritual access" she possessed.

Lydia relates the events of that snowy day with humble grace—determined to make sure everyone who hears it knows it's God's story, not hers.

4

The Meaning of Miracles

WHY DOES GOD CHOOSE TO INTERVENE?

Colson fell!"

When Jeremy Cornett heard his sister Angie's panicked voice on the phone that Sunday morning in April 2005, at first he thought she was probably overreacting. Colson, his son, had recently turned two, and toddlers fall all the time, usually suffering mere bumps and bruises.

Angie had kept Colson and five-year-old Karissa overnight so that Jeremy and Tiffany could have some rare time to themselves. It was a welcome respite from the constant demands of parenting. He wasn't ready to wrap it up to deal with a scraped knee. Besides, Angie was a nurse. *Couldn't she just handle this?*

"You don't understand!" she cried in anguish. "He fell out the *window!*"

Suddenly the floor of the kitchen where Jeremy stood seemed to buckle under his feet. The horrifying reality of what she said penetrated his awareness. He pictured her third-floor apartment . . . and the dizzying distance from her living room window to the ground. It was at least thirty feet, maybe forty. In agonizing clarity, he imagined little Colson leaning over the low-lying sill, then tumbling and falling. . . .

Jeremy, who at that time was not a believer in God—or in anything but partying and reaping the financial fruits of his hard work as a professional chef—sank instantly to his knees. He admits, prior to having kids his lifestyle included plenty of drinking, drugs, and excessive work hours, allowing him to run away from problems. But now, with Angie's terrifying words ringing in his ears, Jeremy had one response: He pleaded with God for all he was worth.

"I don't know how long I knelt there," he said. "All I could do was pray, 'Please, God, give me my son. Don't take my son.' I had only the words I needed, nothing more, nothing less, and I just knew where to turn."

Time seemed to stand still for Jeremy as his wife and grandmother raced around the house frantically preparing to go to Fort Hamilton Hospital in suburban Cincinnati. Then, when paralyzing fear threatened to pull him under completely, he sensed someone standing behind him, just over his shoulder—a warm and comforting presence. He "heard" a voice so clear and strong it might as well have been speaking out loud: *Be concerned. Don't be afraid. Be concerned. He's going to be okay.*

—∞—

Arriving at the emergency room, Jeremy and Tiffany were surprised to learn Colson wasn't there. After some staff confusion that seemed to go on forever, they discovered that the boy was to be flown by medical helicopter to the Cincinnati Children's Hospital, thirty miles away. It was due to touch down momentarily in the spacious parking lot of the Columbia Bowling Lanes, just a few blocks from Angie's place. With luck they could get there before takeoff.

Minutes later, Jeremy drove past the policemen assigned to keep traffic from the landing zone. Ignoring their threats, he had only one thing in mind: to reach the ambulance that held Colson before emergency personnel transferred him to the helicopter.

There was room in the vehicle for only one parent; Tiffany ducked inside first but then quickly reemerged, visibly shaken.

"He's having a seizure!" she cried, barely able to manage her terror. Jeremy climbed in and saw Colson's body, rigid and thrashing, a sign of severe brain trauma known among doctors as "posturing." Devastated by the child's heartrending moans, he put his hand lightly on Colson's chest. Once again, he felt a comforting presence and heard: *Be concerned. Don't be afraid. Be concerned. He's going to be okay.*

When the EMTs announced that they were ready to depart, Jeremy and Tiffany decided to follow by car instead of using space in the helicopter. That would allow room for another paramedic onboard to tend to their son during the flight.

"I walked to my wife's side and put my arms around her," Jeremy said. "She was breaking down, and I knew I had to be strong. I told her he was going to be okay, but I couldn't tell her how I knew. Not yet. I don't know what I said, but I do remember I prayed out loud. For the first time ever, we prayed together."

After liftoff, through grief-stricken sobs, Angie filled in the details about what had happened. Colson was playing in the living room near a window with built-in springs that made it easier to open. She'd raised it an inch or two to allow fresh air inside, but felt it still offered a safe barrier, should Colson go near it.

He did. He bumped into the glass, and the window did as it was designed to do, opening all the way. Instantly tensed yet too far away, Angie helplessly saw the boy lean against the flimsy aluminum screen, which gave way under his weight. She lunged to grab him but was too late.

As if in slow motion, she watched Colson disappear head-first. The ground below was covered in thick juniper bushes—except for a square pad of concrete where an air-conditioner had once stood. He landed there, directly on his head.

"Of all the things I regret about that day," Jeremy recalled, "I'm especially sorry my sister had to see that right before her eyes."

Struggling to control her horror and guilt, Angie quickly described the obvious injuries she observed when she reached Colson: deep contusions on the left side of his head and a grotesquely broken left forearm, bent at a ninety-degree angle.

A seeming lifetime later, the desperate parents arrived at the hospital and were met by a staff member, a soft-spoken middle-aged chaplain. She intercepted them outside the radiology lab where Colson was already undergoing X-rays, a CT scan, and an MRI. The chaplain told them gently what they still hoped might only be a horrible dream: Colson was in exceedingly critical condition.

"That's when it hit me," Jeremy said, "that our son was severely injured and could die. Why else would somebody from the clergy meet us like that?"

He sank to the floor, weeping in overwhelming fear and grief. The confidence he'd maintained evaporated. The possibility that Colson would "be okay," as he'd been assured, seemed to recede over the horizon. He prayed again, *"Don't take my son!"*

Doctors finally reported Colson's grave condition: lacerated spleen, three occipital-lobe aneurisms, brain trauma, seven broken vertebrae, fractured skull, persistent internal bleeding. His head was swollen "like a football." They grimly rated his chance of survival at 50/50, and Jeremy remembers that they consistently added, "But things aren't looking good."

In those traumatic first hours, it didn't occur to Jeremy to ask about his son's broken arm. The other injuries were so serious that the doctors must have forgotten to mention it. Or could the panicked Angie have been mistaken? It didn't matter, anyway. Colson, who still hadn't regained consciousness, was barely clinging to life.

The following three days were a blur of fear, pain, and endless consultations with physicians who did their best to prepare Jeremy and Tiffany for the *best*-case scenario's long road ahead: lengthy hospital stay; months or years of testing and rehab; likelihood of permanent developmental challenges. Colson's condition was perilous; his tiny body lay in a jumble of braces, tubes, monitor wires, and IV lines. Jeremy refused to leave his side for longer than absolutely necessary, even when offered a room at the Ronald McDonald House across the street.

He started a discussion thread asking for prayer at UltimateBass.com, a popular social networking site for sportsmen. "I couldn't believe how many people responded," said the avid fisherman. "In just a few hours word had spread, and Colson had people praying for him all over the world."

On the third day after he fell, Colson was still being kept unconscious because doctors were concerned about bleeding in his brain. After acquainting Jeremy and Tiffany with the various potential risks and complications, they recommended a blood transfusion.

Jeremy was thoroughly exhausted. "I hadn't eaten or slept very much in three days. In a daze, I said I wasn't qualified to decide what was best, so I would agree to whatever they said." Then he found a dark, empty room and lay down. With "Don't be afraid. Be concerned. He's going to be okay" ringing in his ears, Jeremy slept.

———— ⬦⬦⬦ ————

He was jolted awake when somebody on the hospital staff shook him and said, "They need you in Colson's room." What could that mean?

He raced down the hallway, his stomach like an icy fist of dread at the thought of what he might find. He would never be able to forgive himself if, while he slept, unaware, his son had slipped from this life.

The news wasn't at all what he'd feared, though. He was told that the transfusion had been a success, and doctors had opted to discontinue the medication for maintaining a comatose state. As Jeremy entered the room, Colson was showing signs of waking for the first time.

Doctors cautioned that the family shouldn't expect much even if he did regain consciousness. The damage to his occipital lobe would leave him impaired in a variety of ways. Furthermore, it almost certainly ruled out speech function for quite some time.

After a few moments, the boy's eyelids fluttered and opened—and he spoke, thick and slow through the drugs and the swelling: "No, no, no, Daddy . . . you meanie."

"I have no idea what was going through my son's mind at that moment, but I guarantee that was the sweetest sound I'd ever heard," Jeremy said. "Not only did he speak, but he knew who I was. You can't imagine the joy and relief that swept through that room. His mother and I spoke softly into his ear and poured out our tears and love."

Colson wasn't through confounding medical expectations, either. The next day he wanted his favorite sippy cup—"Cuppie!"—and watched *The Adventures of Elmo in Grouchland,* his favorite *Sesame Street* DVD, which Tiffany had brought. His internal bleeding stopped. Four days after falling, he was fully awake and off pain medication.

On day six, Colson left the ICU and was transferred to rehab, where the staff expected him to take months relearning how to walk, talk, use his hands and eyes, even eat. By the eighth day he began walking with no apparent loss of coordination or control. After he pulled the feeding tube from his stomach, the doctors cautiously agreed to let him try solid foods. He then drank ten ounces of PediaSure shake from "Cuppie."

Since Cincinnati Children's Hospital is a part of the University of Cincinnati Medical School, early each morning a professor and a dozen or more medical students crowded into Colson's room, making their rounds. All of them had a copy of his chart and naturally were eager for their mentor's explanation of the boy's remarkable progress.

"I can't tell you how often I heard the words 'I don't know' come out of a doctor's mouth during those days," Jeremy said. "It frustrated them, even seemed to make them mad at times, to have no answer. They knew it had nothing to do with the treatment he was receiving."

Twelve days after plunging more than thirty feet from an apartment window—landing headfirst on a concrete slab and then hovering near death for three days with multiple traumatic injuries—Colson Cornett was discharged without a scratch on his body. Aside from a slight rightward drift in his eyes (which disappeared entirely within two weeks), not a single trace of his brush with death remained. He was given a clean bill of health by the internists, neurologists, and rehab specialists. No one could explain what had just occurred.

⸻⸉⸊⸻

On the way home that day, Jeremy and Tiffany decided to stop at the fire station near Angie's apartment so they could say thank-you. The men assigned there had been the first to respond the day Colson fell. They were at his side just three minutes after Angie dialed 9-1-1.

"We introduced ourselves and told them Colson was the boy they had helped," Jeremy said. "They could hardly believe their eyes. It wasn't long before we were surrounded by several smiling men. We shared the story of everything that had happened and how quickly he progressed while in the hospital."

Then the shock came. A gray-haired man who'd leaned close to examine Colson when they arrived but had remained quiet now spoke up and asked, "What did they do about his arm?"

The question stopped Jeremy in his tracks. He'd completely forgotten about Angie's claim that Colson's arm was broken. The X-rays had revealed no such injury, and the boy's arm showed no sign of any trauma. In the anguish over his condition, and then in hopeful optimism at his remarkable recovery, no one had mentioned it. Until now.

"The man described in detail how my son's arm had been bent backward at a ninety-degree angle at mid-forearm, just the way Angie said. He told me he'd never forget the way the sharp bone was trying to escape the skin from the inside."

And he was adamant. "His arm was *broken*. We splinted it as best we could before the helicopter arrived."

An awed silence came over the young family, and the men gathered around. It was finally interrupted by a young paramedic.

"That's a miracle," he said. "That's *God*."

Jeremy and Tiffany couldn't agree more. Every follow-up test and examination of Colson's progress in subsequent months pointed to the same conclusion: God was true to his word. *"Be concerned. Don't be afraid. Be concerned. He's going to be okay."*

A Closer Look

Why would a God who can do anything that's possible to do, in any way he desires, need to produce miracles? Is there some hidden reason behind what he does, or is it arbitrary? Do people receive miracles randomly, like divine lottery tickets? Or is there a pattern and a plan?

Lots of us love to read stories like Colson Cornett's. And why not? It's a beautiful account of family love and divine protection. At the same time, most people focus on the how, when, and where of such stories, and they don't stop to ask *why*.

We cannot explain why miracles don't happen in all cases (although later we'll discuss that difficult issue). However, it's much easier to explain why miracles *do* happen in other cases. Professor David Weddle notes that "an event that is merely puzzling does not constitute a *miracle* in a religious sense. A miracle is an *interpreted* event, set within a [religious] tradition's broader system of beliefs and understood as signifying something about the transcendent reality."[1]

This expands our definition. We concluded that a miracle is something merely defying *known* laws of nature, something that's observed, yet outside the realm of scientific understanding. Weddle now nudges us a bit further, stating that a miracle also must have an interpretation. In other words, a miracle must have *meaning*.

Decoding Divine Moments

Let's tighten our focus for a moment and highlight the miracles in the Bible. Here are six possible purposes for—that is, meanings of—miracles as found in Scripture:

- To reveal the nature of God, including his love and compassion
- To draw out the faith of diseased people or those in need
- To draw out the faith of those who can help and assist the sick and the needy
- To reveal aspects about Jesus

- To reveal aspects about healers other than Jesus
- To set the stage for a type of showdown ("power encounter") between the forces of good and the forces of evil.

The Old Testament miracles plainly reveal a God deeply in love with his people. They demonstrate the Almighty's providential care and his loving father qualities. Many accounts in both the Old and New Testaments show the importance of the faith of the person or persons impacted by the miracle (for instance, those that peak with statements like "By your faith you have been healed").

In other accounts, the miracle's meaning primarily centers on a compassionate God caring for a distraught person. In fact, one could argue with ease that God's love and mercy is the single most prevailing explanation for the New Testament miracles.

Some stories emphasize an aspect of the conduit through which the miracle happened. A biblical writer might highlight Jesus' role as the Son of God, or as God himself. Some focus on his perspective and experience: One of the two times Jesus is recorded as having wept involved the death of a close friend, Lazarus (whom Jesus raised). He also keenly felt the sorrow of the deceased man's sisters.

Sometimes, faithful servants served as a vessel for the supernatural act: Miracles emanated from Elijah, Elisha, Peter, and John out of their closeness and connection to God.

Professor David Weddle contends that Scripture's miracle accounts are designed not to prove God's existence or power but to reveal his intentions for and relationship to Israel.[2] However, while the biblical miracles truly do reveal and demonstrate that particular divine love, the New Testament gives a broader and far more inclusive picture.

Mark's gospel, presumably the first to be written, emphasizes God's love for *all* people. Matthew also describes numerous miracles. John's narrative sets out to show that miracles proved Jesus to be truly one with God the Father.

Luke hones in on an important question: "How did Jesus do these miracles?" Acts, which is chock-full of supernatural phenomena, provides distinct understanding of the meaning of miracles. The ones in the early church were what John Wimber called "power encounters," events to demonstrate that God is mightier than his adversaries.[3]

Intentional Intervention

Still, we must ask, Can we *always* know the meaning of a miracle?

Well, if we believe Scripture is God's Word and thus our source of truth, and if we're convinced that God is God and therefore never changes, then we can be assured that the reasons miracles occurred in biblical times are the same reasons they occur today.

Miracles do *not* "just happen"—they happen for a purpose. As you consider the stories presented here and other accounts you find elsewhere, inquire, What is this revealing about the nature and traits of God? Was this perhaps done to demonstrate his love and compassion—nothing more, nothing less? Could it reveal a power encounter between good and evil? Is there anything I can learn from it about the person or people involved? Whose faith was impacted by what took place?

Endeavoring to uncover and discover those meanings is fascinating; it's often fun, and it can be fruitful. In the process we'll see that God's decisions have a rationale, even when miracles are delayed or done in a manner no one expected. Whether or not we know what it is, each happens for a powerful purpose.

5

WHAT SKEPTICS SAY

IS IT POSSIBLE TO PROVE MIRACLES?

Dr. Ralph Hatcher, a medically trained professor and self-described "pragmatic man of science," was no stranger to heart attacks. Certainly, as an ER physician, he'd seen more than his share. But heart disease also played a larger role in his life than professional experience, and, in fact, it was deeply personal. His father dropped dead of a massive attack at age forty-nine and wasn't the first man in the Hatcher family to succumb to the devastating disease.

So when Ralph himself had a mild heart attack at forty-two, it didn't come as a complete shock. He was fortunate that the relatively minor event caused little lasting damage to his heart, and he was confident that a proper diet and the right exercise regimen would keep him out of future danger.

"Life goes on," he said. "It was no big deal, then back to business as usual."

For Ralph, that meant more than resuming a daily routine of work and family obligations. It also involved resuming a tepid and tenuous relationship with God—more a matter of long-standing habit than heartfelt conviction. Though his mother was a devout Roman Catholic who'd made sure of his religious education as a boy, Ralph fell away from the faith as a teenager. After leaving home, he served three years in the military, including a tour of duty in the jungles of Vietnam. By the time he returned, his growing attraction to agnosticism essentially had given way to atheism. He started college intending to become a doctor, and he adopted complete trust in science as the ultimate source of wisdom and knowledge.

"Science became my god," he said. "*Reason* held the answers I was looking for, not religion. I believed that anything we don't know yet about how the universe works, we'll learn soon enough through scientific discovery. I even wrote papers mocking faith; I became quite militant for several years."

Thereafter, though, three things would combine to shift his perspective and alter his course: He married Sue, a Christian with a gentle but firm faith; he began medical school, where more advanced study of the human body caused him to doubt whether such elegant complexity really could result from random macro-evolutionary processes; and he endured an episode of profound depression after a crisis that led him to his knees to ask for God's help. He'd come full circle, from childhood belief in God for his mother's sake to personal acceptance of Christ into his life.

Nonetheless, when the crisis eventually passed, Ralph's interest waned. As things returned to normal, he still considered himself a "man of faith," yet in reality this was primarily a label he applied to himself rather than a source of significant identity and an impetus for ongoing growth in his life. He went back to his prosperous practice, re-embraced his preoccupation with material success, and resumed a general indifference toward spirituality.

Until, in 1997, another crisis struck—this time with his very life on the line.

———⚬∞⚬———

Ralph exited the camera shop near his new home in Indianapolis and braced himself once again to face a wintry January afternoon. The blue sky and feeble sunshine were no match for the icy wind that stung his cheeks and eyes. He trotted briskly, eager to finish the last of the errands standing between him and a warm evening at home. The exertion was worth the prize of getting into the car as quickly as possible.

Then . . . *wham*. In a blinding instant, he felt he'd been struck in the chest by a cannonball. Collapsing into his seat, he knew he was having a heart attack. He also knew he shouldn't drive. But with a hospital two miles away, he quickly calculated the time it would take an ambulance to reach him, evaluate his condition, and race him to the emergency room. He turned the key and stepped on the gas.

"By the time I'd been admitted and examined, I felt much better," Ralph recalled. "My vital signs didn't really alarm the doctor, and he told me pretty much what I wanted to hear—it probably was stress-related, no big cause for worry. I'd recently moved to a new city, started a new job, and had four teens at home. It was a plausible explanation."

It would be months before he found out how wrong that assessment truly was.

Some of the "markers" used to evaluate the severity of an attack don't show up in the body till hours later. Had Ralph been kept overnight for observation, the diagnosis would have differed dramatically. As it happened, though, not until the following summer did Ralph begin to notice telltale symptoms: shortness of breath, for instance, and general weakness. He submitted to an updated series of tests, and afterward he knew from the look on his cardiologist's face that nothing about the news was good.

"You had a huge heart attack back there," he said. "Lots of damage."

The bottom line: Ralph was lucky to be alive. An aneurism that had formed in the wall of his left ventricle could have ruptured at any moment and killed him. Surgery was imperative—and soon. He was referred to a specialist, David Heimansohn, MD, who was using a unique revascularization technique that showed good results in cases featuring severe damage. This seemingly routine connection would turn out to be anything *but*.

On Friday, July 11, 1997, Ralph was admitted to St. Vincent's Hospital and spent a quiet night awaiting surgery. His thoughts predictably were filled with uncertainty, but the outlook was good.

The Saturday procedure was a success. Dr. Heimansohn left with his family immediately afterward for a much-deserved break at his vacation home in Michigan. Though Ralph remained in the ICU, all signs pointed to an uneventful recovery.

Then came the evening crash. Ralph's blood pressure "bottomed out," and he hovered perilously close to cardiac arrest—another way of saying "near death," defined as a heart's complete shutdown. His grip on life was slipping, and there was little the staff could do to strengthen it. Now the prognosis was so grim Sue decided to call extended family members, who made plans to travel through the night to be present in the increasingly likely event of Ralph's death.

"I was in and out of consciousness," he said. "I only remember bits and pieces, but I do recall the pain—and the thirst. I was purposely dehydrated to lower the volume of blood in my body and take the load off my heart. Every time I woke, the sensation of thirst was horrible, very intense."

Sunday morning, as Ralph lay awake, staring at the ceiling tiles, he heard distant music that to him at first was indistinct and vaguely amusing. He wondered who was playing music in the ICU of all places. As it grew louder, he recognized the sound of bagpipes, playing a tune strangely familiar, like something he'd heard in a forgotten dream or encountered so long ago that it was more an impression than a memory.

He was about to ask a nurse about this when, from a medical perspective, the worst happened: His heart stopped beating. Cardiac arrest. Technically, Ralph died.

The staff launched into hyperactivity to mount a resuscitation, knowing they had only minutes to succeed. The object of their frantic attention was entirely unaware of it.

"Suddenly I'm standing on a grassy hilltop," he recalled. "I feel fit and strong and wide awake, unlike the semiconsciousness I'd experienced for the past few hours. A lush green meadow rolls downward and away in front of me. To my left stands an old stone wall that follows the contour of the meadow into the valley below. On the right I see a rocky ocean shoreline, with waves breaking gently on gray boulders. The sky is a vibrant, vivid blue, and a refreshing breeze carries the scent of grass and rich earth."

At that moment, Ralph felt as lucid as he'd ever been. The images around him didn't seem surreal, as they often do in a typical dream state. He had no doubt he was truly *there,* wherever that might be. The music was powerful and loud now, and Ralph saw "a man of small stature" strolling away from him down the hill, dressed in a kilt and playing the bagpipes. The song was a pleasant "Irish-sounding" ballad he was certain he'd heard before. Voices sang the melody as the man walked and played.

The scene before him—coupled with his new sensation of vital well-being—filled Ralph with overwhelming peace and joy, like nothing he'd experienced on earth. In an instant he grasped beyond doubt the overwhelming intensity of God's love for him and for the world.

"It's impossible to describe with words what I felt," he said. "Happiness and contentment times thousands and thousands. I remember thinking, *This is what I've been looking for all my life. Everything I've ever done, good or bad, was a step on my journey to this place. All that came before was my attempt to find my way here.*"

Over the next several hours, Ralph "died" and was revived (shocked back) ten times. Each time his heart stopped, he found himself on the same hillside, watching the man walk away from him as he played the wonderful music. Ralph had a burning desire to follow but instinctively knew that if he did he'd be unable to return to life as he'd known it. He was torn between wanting to stay and feelings of responsibility for his wife and children.

"I can't come now," he said aloud to the man. "I'll come with you later."

————— ❧ —————

Later Sunday, Dr. Heimansohn called while on vacation to check on Ralph's condition. Surgeons often work very hard for three weeks straight and then take two off, temporarily leaving all demands as far behind as possible. Learning what had transpired, though, he arranged to return immediately.

While the attending physicians were resigned to accepting Ralph's death, Dr. Heimansohn wasn't ready to give up. In fact, he was the only cardiovascular surgeon in the entire state who still had one more card to play. Furthermore, Ralph lay in the only Indianapolis hospital where that card *could* be played.

Dr. Heimansohn told the family Ralph had one remaining chance: experimental surgery to implant a HeartMate Left Ventricular Assist Device. Approved for use only seven weeks earlier, and used only one time since (with Dr. Heimansohn as the surgeon in charge), ideally it would take over heart function while Ralph waited for a donated organ to become available for transplant.

Sue approved, and the surgery went forward as a complete success. The following day Ralph was awake, with both his blood pressure and heart rate stabilized. Seven months later he received a transplant. Four more months after that he went home and resumed his life, with one notable exception: He no longer takes his faith for granted. Ralph joined a church and remains actively involved.

What to make of the fellow he met in heaven? Ralph's pretty sure he knows. When asked about his ethnic heritage, he doesn't hesitate to answer "Irish"—though he admits the truth is closer to "mongrel," like most Americans who've been here for more than a generation or two. His mother came from the MacDonald clan, and Ralph was particularly close to his maternal grandfather as a boy. He vaguely remembers songs the old man sang, especially after an evening at the corner pub.

"When my mother heard what had happened, she swore the man with the bagpipes was my grandfather come to lead me to heaven," he recalled. "I don't know what any of the images I saw really mean: the man, the hillside, the ocean. The truth is I don't care. What matters to me is that intense *feeling* of love, peace, and happiness. I really believe what I experienced was just a tiny bit of God's love. I'd never felt anything like it before, and I long to have it back now."

In all, Ralph spent 320 days in the hospital, on life support for more than six months total. He could have—should have—died many times. Reflecting back, he's certain God helped him through that frightening and painful experience for a reason.

"I learned to make the best of my life each moment, to make it all worthwhile, to not waste an opportunity," he said. "God gave me a message that he loves me and wants me with him, but also that he respects my autonomy. He gave me a choice that day in heaven: come with me or stay where you are. The real miracle is that I no longer have any fear of death. When it's finally time, I will be ready to go—with joyful anticipation."

A Closer Look

Ralph Hatcher definitely has encountered his share of skeptics and, when he first contacted us, admitted his reticence. Even some Christians said his vision of heaven couldn't have been from God. For the record, we completely believe his account and consider it a true miracle.[1]

The fact is there will always be skeptics when it comes to miracles—or any kind of spiritual experience. There were doubters and detractors thousands of years ago too.

One well-known contemporary skeptic, the stage magician James Randi, who's developed a reputation for debunking paranormal claims, says he'll put his dollars where his disbelief is. For many years he's dangled an enticing challenge: a promised reward of $1,000,000 "to anyone who can show, under proper observing conditions, evidence of any paranormal, supernatural, or occult power or event."[2]

One thing on which we undoubtedly agree: There's a *lot* of phony-baloney when it comes to claims of miraculous powers. If we're going to assert that miracles occur today, we also must acknowledge no shortage of shams and scams. When a man like Randi does expose true fraud, he should be applauded. Still, with so many testimonies to the genuinely miraculous, you may be wondering why, after almost half a century, nobody has ever collected the cash.[3] It's because Randi and his followers have given themselves permission to insist upon certain conditions before accepting a miracle as bona fide:

At the JREF [James Randi Educational Foundation, in Ft. Lauderdale], we design a protocol only after the applicant has clearly stated (a) what they can do, (b) under what conditions, and (c) with what expected degree of success. And, the applicant must find the protocol appropriate, fair, agreeable, and adequate to prove their claim.[4]

Simply put, Randi's interested only in *observable experiments*. All personal testimony, or the accounting of anyone's experience, is irrelevant.

"Cause Unknown"

James Randi has influenced many atheists, including college students like the one we'll call Mac. One day, Mac heard a fascinating claim over the radio.

The show's guest was rock singer Caspar McCloud, star of the Broadway hit *Beatlemania*. But a greater claim to fame would not include New York's bright lights. McCloud was destined to die and come back to life in the presence of many witnesses.

McCloud eventually became a pastor and befriended a faith healer named Henry Wright. Pastor of Pleasant Valley Church in Thomaston, Georgia, Wright invited McCloud to share his testimony and sing at a special service. During the event, though, McCloud suddenly felt so ill he needed to step off the stage. Before it ended, he had a heart attack and fell to the floor.

He had no heartbeat and no pulse; these facts were confirmed by a physician, for McCloud's own doctor had come to hear him sing. She later verified that he'd been dead.

Not one to be taken aback, Henry Wright spoke with the authority of Jesus Christ and commanded Caspar McCloud to come back to life. According to Wright, McCloud's pulse rebounded like an electrical charge. He's alive and well to this day and has written a book about his experience.[5]

In May 2006, McCloud was sharing his story on San Diego's KCBQ when the aforementioned student rang in. Knowing that Mac, a regular caller, was a staunch atheist, the host asked him to respond to McCloud's amazing account.

"I always see a red flag when I hear personal testimonies," Mac replied. "For me to be convinced, we'd need 125 people with a similar heart condition, prayed over in a similar way. Then we would need to evaluate the ratio between those who did and did not come back to life."[6]

This reaction reveals a false assumption about God: namely, that he *always* performs miracles of healing to prove himself. We believe this rarely is the case. Our conviction is that, usually, God's primary purpose for healing a person is to focus on that individual and enhance the relationship.

What's more, although at times God uses miracles to make himself known, he does so in his way and on his terms. We do not originate and administrate or regulate the game plan. Furthermore, bona fide miracles are not replicable or mechanistic—that's what makes them miraculous. God is not a "genie in a bottle" to be called forth at will.

Controlled experiments may prove highly valuable in some scientific fields (like biology or chemistry), but experience is far more interactive than what can be measured in beakers and warmed over burners. One survey found that three-fourths of medical doctors believe in God and that they witness miraculous healings with frequency.[7] However, today's common mindset does not allow their records to contain such words as *miraculously* or *healed*. Expressions like "cause unknown" figure prominently in official reports of unexplainable recovery.

Belief in what can't be empirically tested or proven after the fact requires at the very least some trust, and certainly it necessitates a degree of faith. A person who won't accept even medical reports that don't represent lab testing may be setting himself up for perpetual unbelief.

What Is "Proof"?

Atheists maneuver likewise with historical miracles. The resurrection of Jesus Christ is as verifiable as any event from ancient times. The number of eyewitnesses and historians who reported that Jesus rose from the dead is voluminous. However, author Dan Barker, for example, flippantly dismisses the resurrection account with Carl Sagan's famous quote, "Extraordinary claims require extraordinary evidence."[8] But let's ask this question: How does one verify an historical event?

Suppose you know someone who doesn't believe the American Civil War actually happened in the 1860s. How would you convince her it's a historical fact, when you couldn't repeat the conflict under laboratory conditions with a double-blind study?

You could attempt to find eyewitnesses. Failing that—because everyone who was there is dead—you would seek out someone who knew an eyewitness. Suppose a man in the final skirmishes at age twenty lived ninety years; he could have shared his experiences with someone born in the 1920s who could then share the account with you. You would have accomplished the first task: identifying secondary sources (all the primary sources now would be age 150 or older).

Additionally, you might seek written accounts from 1861–1865 or those penned later by people who had also lived during that time. You could collect the verifiable writings of self-proclaimed eyewitnesses. You perhaps would supplement this with visits to various battlefields, where (if archaeological digs were permitted) you could search for evidence of the weapons used in that time period. Research results in hand, you could make a convincing case for the war's authenticity.

A similar case can be made for the authenticity of miracles. One can walk out onto a stage and perform an illusion; a bona fide miracle, no. "King Herod's Song" in Andrew Lloyd Webber's classic *Jesus Christ Superstar* challenges Jesus to prove he isn't a fool by walking on the surface of a swimming pool. *Superstar* Jesus didn't take the bait, and neither does the real Christ. He's not a carnival huckster, compelled to impress.

One of many reasons the *Infancy Gospel of Thomas*—written long after the actual Gospels—isn't included in the Bible is its portrayal of Jesus as what he was not: a groveling wonder-worker flaunting his powers. To impress his classmates, according to this falsely ascribed[9] document, Jesus "made soft clay and shaped it into twelve sparrows."[10] When one of the children criticized him for "working" on the Sabbath, the boy Jesus supposedly said to the clay birds, "'Go ye, take your flight, and remember me in your life.' And at the word they took flight and went up into the air."

Picture the boy playing with the other kids, shaping clay and then tossing it skyward as the clumps become creatures. Can you hear him muttering, "Whaddya think of that, then, huh?" It's plain that this story runs counter to who Jesus is and what he did.

Jesus began his ministry of teaching and miracles not in childhood but when he was thirty.[11] And he was no show-off.

As *Superstar* correctly portrayed, Jesus Christ had no need to impress Herod. To put it bluntly, he feels no compulsion to "perform" for doubters or scoffers. He's not running a sideshow, and he doesn't dance to their tune when today's skeptics line up alongside King Herod's pool and jeeringly dare him to pony up.

Conversely, Jesus often instructed those he healed to tell no one. Admittedly, his directive proved too hard to keep. Those who were healed did what you and I would have done: They went out and told everyone.

When Peter healed a lame man, the religious rulers demanded to know "by what name" he did it.[12] Apparently a manifestation of God's power didn't occur to them. Even with the proof—the healed man—right before their eyes, the skeptics of New Testament times refused to believe.

All the same, they couldn't refute the result: "Since they could see the man who had been healed standing there with them, there was nothing they could say."[13]

Why Skeptics Are Skeptics

Today's skeptics do their best to refute any claims of the miraculous. Go to *The Skeptic's Dictionary* online and search the word *miracle*. Here's what you'll find:

> Only those who cater to the superstitious and credulous . . .
> would even think of reporting an alleged miracle without taking a very skeptical attitude toward it. No scholarly journal today would consider an author rational if he or she were to sprinkle reports of miracles throughout a treatise. The modern scholar dismisses all such reports as either confabulations, delusions, lies or cases of collective hallucination.[14]

If you believe in a miracle (and happen to write about it), you won't be considered "rational" by the "scholarly." The message is: "*We* are the arbiters of truth. If you say it's miraculous and true, we'll say it's irrational and false. And we are right."

Let's admit something: The miraculous can be hard to prove. As we've said, one cannot take miracles like the ones detailed in this book and recreate them in a lab. Even after examining all possible natural causes and thoroughly vetting those who saw or experienced the allegedly miraculous, it's still difficult to *prove* what happened.

Proof works both ways, though, and even the most dedicated miracle mockers find it equally difficult to prove a miracle did *not* happen. For that matter, neither can they disprove every claim of the supernatural. Take, for example, the existence of God. While it's no easy task to prove that fact, it's no simpler to disprove it, or to demonstrate the actual nonexistence of the supernatural realm.

Want to show that *only* the natural world exists? Know that being unable to perceive something empirically doesn't mean it isn't there. Proving that you've been unable to see, hear, taste, smell, or touch it wouldn't establish that it doesn't exist.

Skeptics say miracles don't or didn't happen because, according to them, miracles *cannot* happen. This brings to mind the story C. S. Lewis told about a woman who said the ghost she saw couldn't really be a ghost, for she didn't believe in ghosts. Circular reasoning demands that we first choose a conclusion and then insist that all evidence be conformed to it.

The evolutionary biologist Richard Dawkins has famously portrayed those who affirm the supernatural as suffering from a "God delusion." In contrast, an atheist "is someone who believes that there is nothing beyond the natural, physical world, no supernatural creative intelligence lurking behind the observable universe, no soul that outlasts the body and no miracles except in the sense of natural phenomena that we don't yet understand."[15]

The obvious presupposition: *Since I don't believe in God, there can't be one.* And, if no God, then no divine acts, no miracles, no supernatural experiences.

Both Belief and Disbelief Demand Faith

Are the stories presented in this book fantasy? Wish-fulfillment? Imagination? We don't think so. Given the facts, the situations, and all the various extenuating circumstances, we believe it takes more faith to deny God than to believe in him. We agree with the title of the book *I Don't Have Enough Faith to Be an Atheist.*[16] Regarding the credibility of eyewitnesses who saw, who observed, who experienced the miraculous, it often takes more faith to prove a miracle did not happen than that it did.

Don't fall under the arrogance of those who say it can't happen and can't be real because you can't prove it. Skeptics, in the interest of integrity, need to admit they're unable to conclusively prove what they affirm. That there's no God and no supernatural realm is simply their belief. As Lewis noted, "If you begin ruling out the supernatural you will perceive no miracles."[17] Begin by assuming the supernatural doesn't exist and that miracles are impossible, and—sure enough—you'll find it impossible to believe.

Many who don't believe in God and miracles insist the burden of proof is on the side of those who do. The truth is we all start on an even playing field as rational human beings attempting to understand a world that's supra-rational. And the affirmation of God's existence or of supernatural activity does not require groundless or eyes-closed faith. The apologist Greg Koukl makes the case that belief isn't about the oft-mentioned "leap of blind faith" but rather an informed "step of trust."[18]

6

"GOD, ARE YOU LISTENING?"

THOUGHTS ABOUT "EARNING" A MIRACLE

Theresa Garner glanced at the clock: It was after five. Randy, her husband, usually was home from work by now. She wondered if he'd been caught in traffic. Not that she had long to ponder it, with a baby and a preschooler vying for her attention.

Jeremiah was five and soon to start kindergarten. He was a natural handful, always racing around and into one thing or another.

Molly was eighteen months and, in some ways, Theresa wished she were *more* of a handful; the blue-eyed toddler was noticeably immobile for her age. Theresa looked lovingly at her daughter, smiling happily on her favorite blanket in the kitchen-corner playpen. Molly had already endured so much.

Diagnosed at three months with cerebral palsy and spina bifida, doctors said she'd never walk. After more than a year of physical therapy, they'd also discovered Molly had been born without a hip socket. If she ever were to achieve the most basic movements, like rolling over or sitting up, she'd soon need extensive reconstructive surgery.

Theresa took a deep breath. It had been a difficult five years for her young family, beginning with the death of their first child, Jasmine, born with even more severe disabilities resulting from a destructive virus Theresa contracted during pregnancy. But God had been faithful throughout, and now, with Molly's operation just weeks away, perhaps things were taking a turn for the better.

She heard Randy's car in the driveway. Moments later he entered the kitchen. Theresa could see immediately that something was wrong.

"Honey, I need you to sit down," he said gently.

Her heart jumped into her throat. "Are you all right? Was there an accident?"

Randy shook his head. "No accident. But I have something to tell you, and before I do, I want you to remember that God takes care of us no matter what."

Theresa pulled a chair away from the table and sat down. She felt numb. Randy was giving her a pep talk *before* delivering the news. It had to be bad.

Then he dropped the bomb. "I don't have a job anymore."

Theresa blinked. "What?"

"I got laid off."

She heaved a heavy sigh. "Oh, Randy, that's awful."

He could see that the full impact had yet to sink in. "Theresa, this means we don't have insurance for Molly's surgery."

They both were in shock. Canceling the procedure wasn't even an option. Without a hip socket, their little girl simply could not function.

They were going to need a miracle.

———— ❦ ————

The couple researched every option. They looked into refinancing their house but didn't have enough equity to make even a small dent; the operation was projected to cost more than $100,000. They spent a lot of time on their knees, asking God to provide the resources they needed to help Molly.

Theresa was secretly bringing another need to God as well. She didn't tell another soul about it: She needed fifty dollars to register Jeremiah for the school they had wanted him to attend in the fall.

In light of everything the family was facing, fulfillment of this desire seemed impossible, even ridiculous. *We can't even pay for Molly's surgery,* Theresa thought, *and here I'm envisioning Jeremiah in private school. What am I thinking?* And yet she quietly clung to the hope that, somehow, everything would work out.

The day finally arrived, and to everyone's relief the operation went exceptionally well. Their surgeon successfully created a hip socket for Molly with bone removed from her other leg. Her prognosis looked good.

Several hours post-surgery, Theresa was still at the hospital when she got a call from Randy, who had returned home.

"I checked the mailbox," he said, sounding puzzled. "There's fifty dollars cash in here with a note that says, 'I know you need this.' I wonder what that's about."

She began to laugh. "Randy, I know *exactly* what it's about! That money's for Jeremiah's school registration. God answered my prayer."

Afterward, she took a deep breath. "Okay, God," she said, "you heard my prayer. Please give me the faith to believe you've also heard our prayers about Molly."

Eight weeks later, Molly's recovery had been slow but steady. Already she had an unprecedented mobility level, and because doctors had used her own bone instead of steel to build her socket, she wouldn't have to undergo more surgery as she got older. While challenges still lay ahead, Molly's new hip would allow her to move around in a manner much closer to normal than anyone had predicted.

One day Theresa said to Randy, "I think it's time to face the music."

For more than two months they had been watching the mail with dread but had yet to receive The Bill. So far, every funding option pursued—retroactive insurance, second mortgages, and so on—had fallen through. It would take decades to pay the whole price.

Randy winced. "I agree. We should call. The sooner we know what we're up against, the sooner we can start whittling it down."

The next day, Theresa rang the hospital.

"You're going to think I'm crazy," she said, "but we need to know when you'll start billing us for Molly's surgery."

"Hold on a moment," the clerk replied. "I'll check your records." When she returned a minute later, she said simply, "Mrs. Garner, the bill's been paid."

Theresa gasped. "What? But how? We have no insurance. There's been a mistake."

A few silent moments passed as the woman examined the records again. "I can't tell you who, Mrs. Garner. It doesn't say. It just says 'paid in full.'"

Her mind raced. She knew none of their friends or family members were wealthy enough to cover the enormous amount. Finally, she asked, "Did the state pay it?"

"Nope. And it just says 'paid in full.'"

"Oh my! The *Lord* has paid that bill for me! Thank you, thank you, thank you!" She hung up and immediately called Randy with the astonishing news.

That was twenty-five years ago. Today, at twenty-seven, Molly functions normally in many ways. The girl whom doctors said would never walk is mobile with a walker and goes to work daily at a vocational center. Her mother describes her as "one of the happiest people you'll ever meet, a beautiful young woman living life to the fullest."

As for Theresa, she believes with all her heart that God is good and gracious. She looks back a quarter century and sees God's undeniable provision, in both the seemingly small and the very big things.

A Closer Look

One of the most pressing questions people ask about miracles is this: "What do I have to do to get God to intervene in my life? Pray harder, believe more, go to the right church, be a better person? *Is* there something I can do to get God's attention so he will respond from heaven?"

When you read a story like Theresa Garner's, maybe you're amazed and inspired. It's especially moving to see how God has provided for a little girl, now a young woman, who's faced such difficult obstacles. When you think of the family's whopping expense being mysteriously and miraculously covered, your heart probably is filled with gladness.

Here's something else that you, along with lots of others, also might think: *How can I get one of those miracles?*

This line of thought isn't surprising, even if most people wouldn't put it quite so bluntly. After all, it sometimes feels as if God hands out miracles arbitrarily and subjectively. We wonder why one person is healed while another in exactly the same situation is not. More difficult to fathom is when people who—from our perspective—don't at all "deserve" God's special intervention receive it, even as faithful servants of God and others appear to be overlooked and neglected.

There's a well-known author we'll call Matt who's written substantially about miracles. Here we want to highlight three of the remarkable stories he tells, about individuals we'll call Dave, Lawrence, and Linda.

One Man's Only Hope

When Dave woke one morning, his aches and pains were worse than usual. It was getting harder even to walk. *A little exercise might do me some good,* he thought. *I'll try to walk for a few minutes.*

When he got outside, though, there was commotion in his neighborhood. People were out on the street, hurrying and scurrying somewhere.

"What's happening?" he asked the first person who slowed enough to hear him.

"He's here—that guy!" She said it as though Dave should know who "he" was.

"Wait!" Dave called. "What guy?"

"The guy who . . ." She paused as if she were out of breath and also unsure of her description. "The guy who . . . who . . . *heals.*"

She took off again.

Wish he'd stop by my place, Dave thought.

He watched the highway-paced foot traffic until curiosity seized him. Then he started hobbling in the same direction.

The two blocks' distance he limped felt like miles. When he finally reached what seemed an unplanned gathering, he saw that the crowd had surrounded a man. *What* man?

Suddenly a burst of confidence shot through Dave's body. He remembered what the lady on the road had said. He wondered whether he might have a chance. Maybe this was his only chance.

Finding just enough strength to push toward the man, Dave cried out, as loudly as he could, "If you want to, you can heal me!"

The others grew quiet. The man saw him. He had *heard*! Softly he replied, "I do want to."

There was a brief pause as their eyes held; to Dave it seemed a decade. "Be clean," said the man.

Dave understood *clean.* It wasn't a matter of "clean" versus "dirty." "Clean" meant *healed,* much like "clean bill of health" signifies wellness to many. The man said it only once, but the words repeatedly echoed through Dave's ears.

Then, to his utter amazement, it happened. He *was* healed.

Completely healed. In shock and wonder, he stared down at his arms, torso, and legs.

And here the narrator abruptly stops the story with an enigmatic statement from the healer, whose name was Joshua: "Don't tell anyone."[1]

A Matter of Authority

But Matt, with a clear intent about to emerge, keeps writing, moving to the next miracle story. He's not just stringing accounts together—he has an agenda. He shifts abruptly to a new chronicle, set in another bustling town, the most prominent one on the north shore of a large lake.

During this time, a foreign government had military personnel stationed there. One of these men, Lawrence, was an officer overseeing a hundred men. Lawrence had a helper, Jason, who was ill; Lawrence believed that a man he'd heard about could cure him, so he went and found that man.

"Shall I come and heal him?" Joshua offered when Lawrence asked.

The man who commanded many said, in so many words, "No need to go all the way to my house. Just order it from here, and your command will be carried out.

"I'm a military man, as you can see. I have soldiers under me, and there are those who rank above me. I know how authority works. When we speak it, those who answer to us obey. I recognize authority when I see it; you obviously have enormous authority. Please use it, and Jason will be well."

Joshua was amazed. "Since you understand authority," he answered, "consider it done, just as you have said. Go home and see for yourself."

Lawrence rushed through the streets at a pace unexpected for a man of his stature. Sure enough, Jason *was* well. Joshua had decreed it, and it happened.[2]

A Touch of Grace

Now Matt quickly shifts focus across town to the residence of a guy named Pete. Although mother-in-law jokes abound, there was no joking about Linda that day. The mother of Pete's wife was gravely ill with a burning fever.

When Joshua walked up to the bed and touched her hand, her temperature dropped to normal. Stunning those who had tried in vain to break her fever, Linda got up.[3]

Three people, with little in common except geographical proximity, had encountered Joshua the healer. All three— Dave, Jason (through Lawrence), and Linda—were restored instantaneously to health. Why did the author of the miracle book choose to tell *these* specific stories? What was his main intent?

If you haven't guessed, these accounts are in the Bible. "Matt" is Matthew, author of the New Testament's first book. We don't know the real name of "Dave" the leper. Regarding "Lawrence," as we called the centurion, we chose "Jason" for his servant, since that name means "the healed one." The large lake was the Sea of Galilee in Israel; the town was Capernaum. "Pete" is the apostle Peter; "Linda" wasn't likely his mother-in-law's name. "Joshua" comes from *Yeshua,* the Hebrew name for Jesus. Why did Matthew include these particular people?

First, lepers were the lowest of the low. Lepers were rejected outright, ostracized from all society. Leprosy meant you lived a distance from everyone else, including your family. Leprosy was like being dead while still breathing. It was the most dreaded of all diseases and represented the most hopeless of all cases.

Matthew's choice to open this section with this account is like raising a bullhorn and announcing across the centuries, "Jesus selected the most despised person to heal. I start with him so that you will know the compassion of Jesus."

Second, Matthew included Jason's account to let us know that Jesus had no healing parameters. There's no way to be outside his borders or beyond his reach.

Yes, Jesus also came for his people, the Jews. But Lawrence and Jason were Gentiles (non-Jews); didn't Jesus realize he was supposed to do nice things only for a select few? There's no missing the message here: You cannot get outside the boundaries of God's love. There are no such restrictions or limitations on his grace.

Third, women in this era were considered property. Gender-blind Jesus, flying in the face of ancient custom, healed a woman, and she certainly wasn't the only one.

Matthew begins this first round of healing accounts—the first of three in his gospel—with a leper, a servant, and a woman. The point couldn't be clearer: Jesus cares for all people. Truly *all*! Jesus shows grace and love to everyone, regardless of status or standing, race or rank. While most things change, some things never do.

There's another point to note as well: Jesus didn't heal people because they deserved it or earned it. He never said, "Pray before every meal and come back in a year. Then we'll see about your miracle." He didn't say, "You've got to clean up your act before I'll make you well." Nor did he say, "You need to be a better person before you'll get my compassion."

Jesus performed miracles freely, graciously, and lovingly.

True, this doesn't explain why some people receive special intervention and others don't. We'll never know that answer this side of heaven, since we cannot know the mind of God. But these stories do provide a powerful principle: We can't merit miracles. We can't win them, warrant them, or work for them. Miracles are given because of who God is, not because of who we are. They are granted because of God's mercy and grace.

Theresa Garner was absolutely right to believe with all her heart that God is good and gracious. It's from those divine qualities, and many others, that miracles are given without respect to who's supposedly deserving and who allegedly isn't.

7

WONDER-WORKERS
AND MIRACLE MAKERS

ARE SOME ESPECIALLY GIFTED TO SERVE AS
CONDUITS OF DIVINE INTERVENTION?

Have you ever heard someone called a wonder-worker or a faith healer? Whatever the medium—TV, on-line, radio, church event, word of mouth—it gets around: Apparently so-and-so did such-and-such with a result that seemingly neither we nor science can explain.

Perhaps a saint, a guru, or an evangelist is credited with a healing or even with raising a person from the dead. What's your initial response when you hear about it?

Very possibly it's the same as ours: healthy skepticism.

It's healthy because we've heard stories about charlatans who take advantage of people, and we want nothing to do with those who defraud and deceive. We also don't want to be labeled naïve or gullible.

We might be intrigued by the possibility that this time it's real. We stand back, though, with a prove-it-to-me mental posture, and well we should. Far too many present-day "miracles" are disproved after the hype and hysteria have died down.

But what if there truly are people through whom God's power flows? And what if they're folks who are just as awed by his decision to perform these wonders as we are? Can a human be *especially* empowered and gifted to perform miracles? If so, why are they specifically chosen for this honor?

We believe that authentic miracles come only from God, who doesn't need to use a person as his instrument. Many reported miracles, however, seem to happen with the help of a man or woman who's apparently a conduit for God's power—a bona fide wonder-worker.

God, of course, is the first recorded worker of miracles, as shown in the creation story. According to Genesis, for a time he remains the only one involved in such miraculous events as the great flood, the burning bush, and the confusion of languages at Babel. When Moses appears on the scene, God chooses to use a human helper, as recorded in the book of Exodus.

Of the more than one hundred miracles recorded in the Bible (including fulfilled prophecy), most can be attributed to a person in whose life God intervenes.[1] Still, only a handful of biblical characters witnessed miracles coming through their unique touch.

Early Miracle Makers

Moses and his brother, Aaron, had the difficult task of demonstrating God's power and authority before a cynical and belligerent Egyptian ruler. Together they performed ten miracles, culminating in the death of every Egyptian firstborn son. The same narrative records Pharaoh's court magicians performing miracles of their own, and whether these were authentic miracles emanating from darker powers or simply magic tricks, we don't know.

Moses goes on to perform several other miracles hand-in-hand with God—parting the sea, for example, and producing water from a rock. Throughout the book of Exodus, however, God's voice is clearly heard and his hand seen; sometimes Moses doesn't appear to be involved in the miraculous at all (such as with the provident pillar of cloud in the desert).

Still, the addition of Moses as a player in these events is significant: God chose for the first time to partner with a human who would both proclaim *and* demonstrate his awesome power. God selects Moses to do *something,* even if it's merely stretching out his hand when God directs. Since the power behind the miracles comes from above, Moses doesn't need to conjure up any qualifications or competence. He just needs to be obedient to the higher authority.

This minor human action provides a clue to what's coming: God is going to put the spotlight more and more on miracles happening through *people.* Kenneth Woodward, in *The Book of Miracles,* observes that this shift represented more than a movement from God as the "agent" of miracles to humans serving in this role. There is also a change in the visibility level.

From Moses to Elijah, miracles are performed by individuals (as God's agents), but only before groups. That is, they are *public* miracles. With Elijah and Elisha, miracles are for the first time performed by individuals for individuals. That is, miracles became increasingly *private*.[2]

Further, the miracles through Moses, Joshua, Elijah, and Elisha set the stage for what's to come later: the New Testament focus on Jesus and his followers as conduits for miracles.

This isn't at all to say that God the Father disappears from the miracle business. Jesus, front and center as *the* miracle worker, stresses that he only works as he sees the Father working. His closest friend, John, quoted him on this: "Very truly I tell you, the Son can do nothing by himself; he can do only what he sees his Father doing, because whatever the Father does the Son also does."[3] Thus the human form (conduit) was still directly tied to God's power.

Some of Jesus' followers performed or experienced miracles after he returned to heaven. Peter healed a paralyzed man,[4] and Paul was freed from prison by a perfectly timed earthquake.[5] But what about after the New Testament era— did miracles cease then? Some say yes, that the age of miracles ended with the deaths of the apostles. However, historical writings indicate that this is incorrect.

Irenaeus, in *Against Heresies* (c. AD 185), claimed that inexplicable things continued after that time.[6] Augustine of Hippo (354–430), early Christianity's most influential thinker, originally believed miracles ceased with the New Testament period yet changed his opinion in the end after scrutinizing and recording miracles in a revival that broke out across Northern Africa.

The Venerable Bede (672–735), one of the faith's early historians, wrote the classic *Ecclesiastical History of the*

English People (731). This work is so saturated with miracles that it broaches the conclusion that such events were widely reported, at least among English Christians, in the eighth century.

The record doesn't stop there. For instance, miraculous phenomena were associated with

- Bernard of Clairvaux (1090–1153)
- Hildegard of Bingen (1098–1179)
- Dominic (1170–1221)
- Francis of Assisi (1182–1226)
- Anthony of Padua (1195–1231)
- Clare of Montefalco (1268–1308)
- Bridget of Sweden (1303–1373)
- Vincent Ferrer (1350–1419)
- Martin Luther (1483–1546)
- The "French Prophets" (1685–1710)[7]

The sixteenth-century reformers, like Martin Luther and John Calvin, were far less concerned with defending the authenticity of the supernatural than with demonstrating that many so-called medieval "miracles" had been based on false beliefs that held the church in bondage to superstition. Charlatans *were* influencing those who lived in ignorance then, just as they've done throughout subsequent ages. All the same, authentic miracles hadn't disappeared.

Additionally, in a letter to Thomas Church in June 1746, John Wesley, England's influential revivalist, asserted that miracles were still occurring.

I do not know that God hath any where precluded himself from . . . working miracles in any kind or degree, in any age, to the end of the world. I do not recollect any scripture wherein we are taught that miracles were to be confined within the limits . . . of any period of time.

Johann Blumhardt had a normal if not mundane ministry as a German Lutheran pastor until 1842, when he experienced an outpouring of miracles that followed a successful exorcism. Also affected were the people of his town, Möttlingen, an obscure village in southern Germany. "It was claimed there were many healings, conversions of some of the church's most determined opponents and radical transformations of life and character."[8]

While most people are aware of miracles happening in biblical times, many fail to recognize that miraculous occurrences have been recorded in virtually every age. The record of God's miracles stretches from ancient times until today.

Miracle Workers in Modern Times

Stepping into more recent times, to locations and names more familiar, in late-1920s Los Angeles, cynics would become believers at the architecturally breathtaking Angelus Temple, which seated well over five thousand. Ambulances lined up to bring the sick to be prayed over by Aimee Semple McPherson (1890–1944). Year after year people witnessed miracles despite a long-running rash of rumors pertaining to the evangelist.

Followers of A. A. Allen (1911–1970), an evangelist whose life was less than exemplary, reportedly experienced numerous miracles at his services. Allen was inspired to start a ministry after attending an Oral Roberts tent meeting in 1949.

Many said they were miraculously healed by the controversial yet highly regarded Katherine Kuhlman (1907–1976), whose ministry was known around the world for decades.

Few reports are more astounding than those involving Smith Wigglesworth (1859–1947), an Englishman who focused on faith healing. He's reported to have been instrumental in such miracles as blind eyes seeing, deaf ears hearing, cancers disappearing, *and* fourteen people being raised from the dead.[9]

So massive was the outpouring of miracles and healings in Gordon Lindsay's ministry that the Dallas-based evangelist (1906–1973) founded a monthly magazine, *Voice of Healing*, dedicated solely to recording these events. His son, Dennis, carried on his father's tradition with the supernatural.[10]

Oral Roberts (1918–2009), founder of the university in Tulsa that bears his name, reported seeing untold numbers of people healed through his prayer and touch. He's known for saying people must understand that "*God* heals, I don't."

Regardless of the character flaws and individual failures among some of these very public figures, there's no dispute that many people—including some we know personally—claim to have been miraculously healed from years of pain, sickness, and suffering through their ministries. There's also no denying that those who have had a healing experience remain forever grateful.

Almost all these faith healers have shared a common concern: Like Roberts, they've wanted it known that they themselves couldn't heal anyone. On their own, they wouldn't produce a single miracle. Many of the best known among them have gone to great lengths to help people realize that only God brings healing.

I (Jim) studied the healer John Wimber (1934–1997) and personally saw evidence of miraculous healings at his purposefully unsensational services. Wimber disallowed what he called "mood music," concerned that it would artificially foster an emotional environment. He refused to make claims regarding healing as he finished praying for people; in fact, he insisted they not claim they had been healed until they could get to their physicians for medical testing, and only then—after medical confirmation—did he regard a healing as bona fide. Wimber took a rational approach to the process, aiming to dissociate from manipulation and attempting to catalogue data to analyze it for identifiable patterns. Due to his strong intellectual bent, he encouraged careful scholarship, inviting students to research what was happening.

A God-Given Gift

Among the many gifts or unique abilities that God gives to his children, one catches our attention here. This is what Paul, in 1 Corinthians, calls "miraculous powers," and he mentions "gifts of healing" just prior.[11] It's clear that God gives the ability to perform miracles or deliver healing to some and not to others.

If you find this amazing or perplexing, you aren't alone. Many of history's most well-known healers seemed genuinely puzzled at (and could not precisely explain) the miracles that have flowed from their ministries. If these human conduits did not have a perfect understanding of their own gifts, we might have even more difficulty explaining how miracles happen.

Even so, while we may not fully comprehend why and how God chooses to work through certain individuals, we can't deny that he did in centuries past and still does today.

In the pages that follow, we want to shine the spotlight on a remarkable woman who had a remarkable journey toward healing. Was she skeptical about people who claimed to have special powers? Absolutely. Until . . .

Modern-Day Miracle: Just One More Prayer

On Sunday evening, June 8, 2003, Vonna Wala sat next to her husband, Phil, about three-quarters of the way back from the altar. Fading sunlight filtered softly through the stained-glass windows of the historic sanctuary their congregation had leased from a nearby Lutheran church.

The Christian Assembly in Waseca, Minnesota, was like a second family to Vonna, an oasis of service and comfort among people she loved. That night, though, the dark wooden ceiling arching high above white plaster walls and burgundy carpeted floors felt like foreboding clouds amid pre-storm stillness. She sat with her arms folded tightly across her chest, shielding herself against a bitter disappointment with which she'd become well acquainted.

To her, *hope* was fast becoming a frayed and threadbare word, one she was almost ready to abandon for good. For four years she'd fought a losing battle with an advanced and aggressive form of multiple sclerosis. After fruitlessly seeking divine healing again and again, perhaps it was time, she thought, to accept that it was her fate to remain sick and crippled.

The minister that evening was a guest speaker, a man who specialized in healing services. His central message was one Vonna had heard all too often recently: that healing is available to anyone at any time. If one isn't healed, he said, the reason may lie within. Unconfessed sin or deeply held judgments, for instance, can thwart God's desire for you to be well and whole.

"To tell the truth, I didn't really like his preaching style and didn't necessarily agree with everything he said," Vonna recalled. "I've always resisted the idea that if you're sick it's because there's sin in your life or things blocking you from getting well. The last thing a sick person needs to feel is guilt. Besides, I'd already been up there five hundred times for healing prayer. I told God, 'I'm not going again.'"

But Phil gently encouraged her to try at least once more. What did she have to lose? When the call finally came, she stood and, leaning on her cane, made her way slowly to the front, where she joined six or seven other seekers in line.

"It was an act of obedience, not of faith," she said. "I was hanging on by my last three threads."

When it was her turn, Vonna quietly told the minister of her condition. She choked up with tears as she shared the story of the pain she'd suffered and the treatments she'd endured—including chemotherapy and intravenous steroid injections—all with little or no lasting effect. She told him of being forced to abandon her dream of licensed family counseling . . . of fatigue stalking her every day, stealing her ability to care for her family and for others as she always had . . . of the frustration she experienced just walking across the floor and being afraid of falling.

In his eyes, she could see genuine compassion. He listened, he placed his hand gently on her head, and he prayed.

"I honestly don't remember what he said," Vonna recalled. "But I remember feeling a quiet sense of peace come over me, nothing astonishing or dramatic. I'd been working to overcome resentments I'd carried my whole life toward my alcoholic father and others in my family. I felt like all that just melted away, and I was finally at peace."

Then, still leaning on her cane, still unable to lift her left foot properly, still a person suffering from MS, Vonna returned to her seat.

Vonna's path to the altar that night started in May 1999, when she noticed a spreading numbness on the left side of her body. Initially she thought the sensation was related to two previous back surgeries, but doctors, suspecting more, ordered an MRI of her brain, since an aneurysm was one of the conditions that might account for her symptoms. The test was inconclusive, though MS was among the possible culprits her physician mentioned.

In June, she underwent a series of follow-up tests at the Mayo Clinic: a spinal tap, additional brain scans, and nerve-response evaluations. The result was not encouraging, for the diagnosis was "lab-supported suspicion of MS."

"It was only called 'suspicion' because I hadn't yet had at least three previous flare-ups," she said. "But all the evidence pointed there nonetheless."

Through the remainder of 1999, Vonna's flare-ups became more frequent, and her list of symptoms grew to include pain in her eyes, blurred and double vision, dramatic loss of energy and motor function, and flashes of pain down her left side like electrical jolts. She began to experience "foot drop" and inability to lift her left leg normally when she tried to walk.

In January 2000, when she consulted one of the Midwest's top MS specialists, her fear was confirmed: relapsing/remitting multiple sclerosis, the most common form, in which symptoms may come and go for many years.

By spring 2001, her condition had worsened vastly, and she no longer recovered fully between relapses. Accordingly, her diagnosis was changed to a form of the disease in which symptoms progress rapidly and aggressively. She was fitted with a leg brace so her foot wouldn't drag and cause a fall. She underwent an experimental chemotherapeutic treatment using Novantrone, an immune system suppressant that interrupts degenerative action. It worked well—for a time. Then her symptoms invariably returned.

By October 2002, Vonna was deemed permanently disabled and began depending on an electric wheelchair nearly all the time. The couple had little choice but to move from the beloved split-level home they'd just renovated into a house with no stairs. Vonna closed down her supervised counseling practice though she was halfway to completing state requirements for becoming a licensed therapist—a cherished dream she felt God had led her to pursue. Years later, her doctor confided that out of hundreds of patients, she was one of just a handful he dreaded seeing on his calendar because he'd run out of therapies to try. They'd done everything he could think of, and still her condition worsened.

"It was all I could do to go to the grocery store and do a load of laundry on the same day," she said. "My brain was wide awake, but many times I was so tired I couldn't even move my body as I lay on the bed. The hardest part was to feel so helpless. I'd always done things for other people. Suddenly I was the one who needed help, and that was hard for me to take."

In June 2003, Vonna planned to visit her sister in Washington State. They were to stay in a cabin on San Juan Island, north of Seattle, but she warned her sister not to expect much sightseeing from her; she'd likely spend most of the ten days sleeping and reading as usual. Phil and the kids would follow a few days later.

When scheduling the trip, Vonna decided to wait until June 12 for departure so she could attend a series of special meetings at church. It wasn't often they had guest speakers and she felt it would be wrong not to participate.

At ten o'clock on June 8, after Vonna and Phil had returned home from the evening service, she was fatigued and went to bed first. As she stretched out, barely able to move after an exhausting day, she fell into a quiet, meditative state, hovering between wakefulness and sleep.

"I suddenly felt a soothing warm sensation that started at the top of my head, moved across the left side of my face, and continued all the way down the side of my body. It felt like being lowered into a hot, steamy bath. It was so gentle, and it lasted about five minutes. I've never felt anything like it before or since, but I knew immediately it was God."

She called to Phil from the bedroom: "I think God's healing me!"

Phil hardly knew what to say. For four years he'd struggled with his own doubts and difficulties. He felt it was his role to be encouraging but also realistic. He was a skeptic by nature and had seen similar things many times: someone goes up for prayer and swears he's been healed of something or another—then a week later he's right back where he started.

"When she yelled from the bedroom that God was healing her, I said, 'That's great,' but I was really thinking, *How am I going to deal with the disappointment tomorrow morning when she's back to her old self?* I was trying to be supportive, but honestly I just felt helpless. I was protecting myself by being guarded."

The next morning, Vonna felt great. After Phil went to work, she walked around the house with more energy than she'd felt in years. *Just a good night's sleep?* she wondered. She drove to a nearby Wal-Mart, parked in one of the handicapped spaces by the entrance, and headed inside. Before reaching the door, she rang Phil.

"I'm having trouble walking," she said.

Phil thought back to the night before and hesitated, not knowing how to respond.

"I *mean*, my left leg is working again, but I'm having a hard time remembering how to walk normally."

Still not daring to believe her improvement was permanent, everyone went about their normal routine until Wednesday, when Vonna left for Washington. Each night while away, she would call home to report all she had done: hiking for miles around scenic hills; kayaking out into the sound to watch orca whales up close; more hiking to visit a nearby lavender farm . . . things that suddenly weren't out of the question. By the time her family arrived, they all were ready to admit that something astonishing had occurred.

"When Vonna met us at the airport," Phil said, "I remember distinctly that we went to a restaurant for dinner. She was walking a little ahead of me and the kids toward the entrance. It was so wonderful to watch her walk briskly and without a limp, we just stood back grinning at each other. That's when it really hit me that God *had* done a miracle."

One month later, Vonna returned to see her doctor, whose reaction was stunned disbelief. He was unable to detect the slightest hint of what had been one of the most aggressive cases of MS he had ever treated. He could only say, "It's a miracle," and could come up with no reason why she needed to take any more medication for MS.

Vonna Wala got her life back, and it was by no means identical to the one she'd watched slip away over the years of her illness. She completed her education and became a licensed family therapist. She resumed her active life of service at church. Along the way, too, she lost the prideful attachment she'd once had to those things. She learned to relax and enjoy life's little moments, no longer taking for granted God's daily gifts.

"I'd always been more of a human *doing* than a human *being*. Before I got sick I was Miss Energizer Bunny, always compelled to fix everything and everyone. That's not true anymore. The illness forced me to let go and let God be in charge.

"I have no idea why he healed me and not others. But I do know it had nothing to do with how hard I worked. It was pure *grace*."

8

GOD'S FAVOR OR GOOD FORTUNE?

COINCIDENCES DO HAPPEN.
SO DOES DIVINE INVOLVEMENT

Y ou've probably heard a tale like this, maybe more than once: The person delivering the report—whether a friend, family member, an acquaintance, even a stranger—mesmerizes her audience with vivid detail and sometimes hair-raising suspense. You can't doubt it's true because it happened to the storyteller herself.

She completely lost control of the travel van, which veered off the road and plunged over the embankment, rolling repeatedly. The crashes of metal against boulder were deafening.

At the bottom, the vehicle was crushed like a tin can. Almost everything that had been inside was now strewn all over the creek bed.

Stunned and in shock, she began to check on her six passengers, expecting the worst. Instead, to her astonishment, she found everyone alive *and* uninjured.

As she dramatically recounts the heart-stopping specifics for the five-hundredth time, five years afterward, the driver concludes with the same expression she's shared again and again: "It was a *miracle*!"

You nod in agreement.

In fact, most people would agree, maybe without giving it much thought, "Yes, that really was miraculous."

But we'll be honest. Instead of thinking, *How great that God intervened to save their lives!* we might be wondering, *Why didn't he just keep them from careening off the road in the first place? That would have saved even more headaches and spared a van.*

Don't get us wrong. We believe in God, and we believe in his miracles. We also don't pretend to have all the answers, especially when it comes to life's big mysteries. Thankfully, God is so secure that he's untroubled when we raise such questions.

So again, restated: If God obviously meant to spare those lives, why not prevent the accident itself? Or, if he's capable of keeping something horrible from happening (and he is, or he wouldn't be God), then why doesn't he?

Journalist Martin Bashir asked this question in a much more challenging and sophisticated way on a recent national news program. Speaking to a well-known pastor about a natural disaster that caused thousands of deaths, Bashir said, "Either God is all-powerful but he doesn't care about the people of Japan and therefore their suffering, or he does care about the people of Japan, but he is not all-powerful. Which is it?"[1]

Frankly, it was an embarrassing moment for this megachurch pastor, as well as for many people of faith watching.

Apparently taken aback by the question, the pastor bobbed and weaved like a stunned fighter on the ropes. His vague reply, about a God who cries when we cry, offered nothing of substance; it was a non-answer.

How would you have answered the question? The correct response is: neither option. Bashir had boxed in the pastor, but this otherwise quick-thinking, skillfully glib preacher didn't address the fact that he had just been given two false choices. The answer is that *both* statements are wrong.

While the all-powerful (omnipotent), all-loving (omni-benevolent) God wants nothing but good for his creation, and while he designed all whom he created to experience exactly that, there also is another spiritual being who, though not all-powerful, acts in opposition to all that is good, striving unceasingly to wreak havoc through evil.

God—in his power *and* love—created a perfect world. He likewise gave us humans the capacity or ability to choose how we respond to him. He did this because he wants decision-driven love (the only kind there is), not automatic or robotic obedience.

With the power of volition comes the freedom to choose wrongly. Humankind began doing that when Adam and Eve opted to trust their own situational decisions instead of God's wise directives.

In addition, Satan, who once had been the most breath-taking of all the angels, had rebelled against his Maker. As the initial source of evil, he offered Adam and Eve the opportunity to join his rebellion. They chose against God, and as a result our world suffered a massive loss of excellence. A cycle of decay infiltrated what had been a paradise,

117

bringing heartache, suffering, sickness, catastrophe, and death.

The present state of imperfection, including all that's wrong with the world, will persist until God fulfills his promise to reinstate our reality to flawlessness. That day is not yet here, and temporarily we live in a fallen place that staggers from one man-made or natural disaster to another.

Thus the terrible things that happen: diseases, floods, wars, earthquakes, crimes, hurricanes, famines, betrayals, tornadoes. Whether it's an accident that impacts one family or a volcanic eruption that devastates a region, we find ourselves wondering where God is during the tragedy.

Is God powerful but heartless? No.

Is God loving but impotent? No.

God, who *is* love and who lacks nothing, so values our freedom—which, again, is intrinsic to love—that he allows creation to reap the time-bound results of our choices even as he guarantees that, in the end, he'll restore his handiwork to eternal perfection.

But what about our original question, the one as to why, even though God miraculously spared lives *in* the accident, he didn't spare their lives *from* the accident?

The answer is that, as with Martin Bashir's dilemma, the premise is wrong. God does not stage the ills that plague our existence; these are the natural consequences of a broken world. Instead of wondering why God isn't preventing this conflict or eliminating that malady, we need to be asking why the devil chose to bring about evil . . . why he wants to "steal and kill and destroy"[2] . . . why Adam and Eve determined to bring such suffering upon themselves . . . why we so frequently make self-destructive decisions . . .

why we're willing to injure or deprive others to get what we want.

Furthermore, despite all those causes of hardship and pain, God *still* intervenes, often keeping us safe from disaster and anguish. Ultimately it isn't "Why don't you do more, God?" but rather "I'm amazed at how very much you have done!"

Best of Luck or God's Benevolence?

When a positive outcome occurs—a child is resuscitated after a near-certain drowning, or a man survives a massive stroke— how do we know if it's direct divine intervention or merely great luck? Genuine miracle or nature taking its course?

The straightforward answer is we don't always know. At the same time, there's a basic principle that can guide our thinking.

When something happens for which there is no discernable or observable explanation, it's not irresponsible to "see the hand of God," who works in myriad ways and to varying provisional degrees. However, even as we ask legitimate questions and make educated guesses, we needn't presume which acts of God qualify as *miracles*. As we've said, divine intervention could range from simple answered prayers through the unmistakably miraculous.[3] More important, the line between "bona fide miracle" and "providential coincidence" often blurs.

Recently I (Jim) received an unexpected call from a highly respected, nationally renowned specialist who, within fifteen minutes of learning the seriousness of my wife's condition,

119

had arranged for her to be taken to Houston's MD Anderson Cancer Center, a top cancer hospital. Through this connection, we got an appointment when there were otherwise no openings.

Was that a miracle? No, even though it certainly was good fortune. This physician is a friend of, and in proximity to, a politician we both know.

However, becoming a friend of the politician in the first place was a fluke. And prior to that there was another fluke. A fluke behind that too. If I could share the entire story here in sequential steps, you would probably say, "What are the chances that *all* those events would come together?" The odds actually are very long.

That out-of-the-blue call itself? Probably not a miracle. The series of surprising events that led up to it? Honestly, I can't say with certainty. But because our arrival at MD Anderson came about from the confluence of so many improbable elements, the cumulative total of "unlikelys" leads me to believe a miracle did occur in our lives.

You might know someone who invokes the "It's a miracle" expression at everything positive: a job promotion comes through, a given-up-for-lost earring turns up under the couch, a risky investment turns a profit. It's possible that person means "This is wonderful—thank you, God!" Probably he or she doesn't mean an actual supernatural occurrence.

Other people use the term in a general sense, speaking of the "miracle of life" when a baby is born or exclaiming of a "miraculous sight" at a vibrant sunset on the horizon. Most pointedly they're acknowledging the greatness of God's creation.

There are those also who usually talk of *luck, chance,* or *fate* when favorable events unfold. They may say the "planets are aligning" or their "lucky stars are shining." Yet we deny the reality of a providential God when we fail to recognize his hand on us in unpredictable and inexplicable ways. In the "God or good fortune" question, we'd exchange "good fortune" for "being blessed by God."

So was it God, or was it being blessed by God?

Answer: both.

Consider the story of Arvid Metcalf, whose near-tragedy easily could have cost him his life. Some people probably heard of Arvid's experience and said, "Wow, was he *lucky!*" or "What a *fortunate* man to have survived." In this case, we say, "Sounds like a miracle to us." Your turn to decide.

Modern-Day Miracle: "Biology Suspended"

When Arvid Metcalf got out of bed on Wednesday morning, November 1, 1978, he, like most other residents of Lexington, Kentucky, was unaware that far beneath his feet a battalion of workers with heavy machinery was on the job. They were there because this part of the world was once covered by a shallow sea that slowly had formed hundreds of feet of high-quality Ordovician limestone.

Over the years miners had burrowed deep under the city to quarry the rock. Each afternoon they used explosives to turn solid stone into rubble; crews spent the night and morning hauling it to the surface, clearing the way for further blasts. Tunneling underground allowed the process to continue around the clock, in any weather. It also permitted a major mining operation to coexist with a large urban population, unnoticed.

Well, almost.

Arvid and his wife, Judy, owned and operated a small plumbing company that was subcontracted to install a sewer line in an under-construction housing development. The ordinarily routine task involved digging a relatively shallow ditch for laying pipes. But two facts conspired to make that day's job anything but ordinary.

First, because sewer lines drain by gravity, the outflow end must be lower in elevation than the inflow. This site's topography rose steadily toward outflow—meaning the ditch had to run ever deeper beneath the surface to maintain the proper slope.

Second, a specialized machine belonging to the general contractor, one designed to "lay back" ditch sides sufficiently to prevent a cave-in, was out of service that day. Instead, the company provided a large backhoe that dug a ditch sixteen feet deep and only two feet wide. Plus, proximity to nearby trees and the property boundary would have severely complicated the process of widening the ditch enough to meet safety standards.

"It was an unsafe ditch, to say the least," Arvid recalled. "I'd promised Judy when we started the company I'd never go into a ditch like that, but the general contractor's people had more experience, and they said the tree roots would hold it. We went ahead."

Arvid worked in shifts with his employee, Greg Lippman, taking turns at the bottom. As they finished a section of pipe, the backhoe operator above would cover it with dirt, creating a ramp for Arvid and Greg to enter and exit the ditch. Late in the afternoon, Arvid started down the ramp, calling to Greg that it was time to switch.

Somewhere in the man-made caverns far below, engineers had carefully placed explosives into the leading face of a tunnel that probed deep into the ancient limestone. Occasional fossils were the only reminder that the rock had once been soft sediment on the earth's seafloor.

They performed the necessary safety checks on the equipment. They tested the circuits of the detonator. Then, at exactly 4:30, like he'd done many times before, a crew member activated the switch.

As always, the distant explosion was so faint at the surface that no one working up there noticed it. Yet the silent shockwaves were strong enough to unsettle a precarious balance in the towering trench walls.

"I'd started back down the ramp," Arvid said, "and Greg was walking toward me, still in the deepest part of the ditch. Suddenly I saw one of the walls start to fall in, like dominoes, in big blocks. I ran toward Greg, thinking I could shield his head from the falling dirt, but the whole thing went before I could reach him, and it got us both."

When the cave-in finally stopped, Greg was buried beneath ten feet of heavy clay dirt. Arvid was covered by four feet.

One of the workmen raced to a nearby house, burst through the door without knocking, and asked to use the phone. He informed the dispatcher, then added, "If you're still listening to me, you're wasting time."

Emergency responders wasted none and were on the scene in minutes. A fireman with backhoe experience took the controls while others knelt and searched around with their hands ahead of the heavy bucket for Arvid's hardhat. It was a sprint against time, but one they had to run with extreme caution. The two great fears of the rescuers were causing additional damage to the walls and further injuring the buried men.

Meanwhile, Arvid was completely conscious and aware. Immobilized by the earth pressing on him, he assumed he'd soon be dead. He knew very well his chances of surviving this were slim. He would rapidly run out of any residual air trapped with him—little indeed, judging from how the dirt was tightly packed around his face and *in* his nose and ears. He also knew the rescue itself was a dangerous undertaking. "I'd heard stories about cave-ins where they'd come up with the guy's head in the bucket of the backhoe."

Still, he felt remarkably calm and peaceful. As a Christian, he wasn't afraid to die. He felt guilty for allowing work to proceed in an unsafe environment when he could have put a stop to it. He was sorry he'd broken his promise to Judy. He regretted that his poor decision-making had likely cost Greg his life as well. He thought of his daughters, then ages seven and eight, but he knew God would care for them. He was thankful for the life insurance policy that would provide for his family now. He told God he was ready to go.

And time went by. After what seemed like an eternity, he could tell the rescuers were getting closer. He tried to yell each time he felt backhoe pressure over his head. At 5:02, after being buried thirty-two minutes, Arvid saw the waning light of day when firemen gently uncovered his head.

He still couldn't breathe, and when they realized he was bent at the waist, they immediately freed his chest and arms.

Standing up straight, Arvid took his first breath in over half an hour.

After a bit more digging, they cut off his pants at the knees and tugged him out of his still-buried boots. An ambulance waited as he said exactly where to find Greg.

"If I hadn't been down there too and seen where Greg was when it started, they wouldn't have known where to look for him," Arvid said. "The ditch had been open at the bottom for about thirty feet, and no one else would have known where he was."

Incredibly, Arvid wasn't injured. He was released from the hospital after an hour of observation, just to ensure he wasn't in shock. While there he heard the astonishing news: Sixty-two minutes after the cave-in, rescuers had reached Greg—and he was *alive*.

"When they let me out, I went straight back to the scene," Arvid said. "There were TV news crews everywhere and big floodlights, because it was dark by then. They had built a plywood shelter around Greg and were giving him an IV, but he was alive."

Because of the constant danger of further collapse, it was past two a.m. before they finally pulled Greg free. He'd suffered a broken collarbone and ankle.

"People always ask me if there'd been a pocket of air trapped with us, to explain how Greg and I survived being buried for so long," Arvid said. "But that's not what happened. I had dirt in every orifice—there was no pocket. That heavy, dense dirt was packed around my entire body. It was a suspension of the normal laws of physics and biology. It was a miracle."

125

Not long after the accident, Arvid returned to his first love: aviation. But his brush with death in the Kentucky soil has stayed with him through the years. He no longer worries about the "small things in life" and considers every day a "free day." Each moment is a gift God gave on the day he should have died—but inexplicably didn't.

9

POWERFUL PROMPTINGS

WHEN GOD SPEAKS TO US IN A
STILL, SMALL VOICE

On August 19, 2010, Janet Glaser of San Diego felt a strong urge to pray for a hedge of protection around her children and grandchildren. A firm believer in prayer, she frequently asked for God's hand of safety and security to be on her family members. This time, though, the deep-down impulse she experienced felt urgent and pressing.

Not aware of anything dangerous or risky occurring, she nevertheless prayed fervently, and she clearly sensed God's presence. Two days later, Janet's oldest daughter, Sandy—living two thousand miles away—found herself in great need of protection.

———

In the sudden blue glare of lightning's flash, a thicket of rain-drenched oak trees leapt out through the blackness, thrashing in the wind as if to warn Sandy Rupp of the danger ahead. She'd spent the evening at her friend Ellen's remote cabin in the wooded hills outside Warrenton, Missouri. Thunderstorms had dumped torrential rains in slow-moving squalls all afternoon and into the early evening.

Seated behind the wheel of her Honda CRV, she glanced at the time—10:50 p.m.—and dialed her husband, Gale, to let him know she was headed home. Sandy wasn't worried; the rainfall had gradually softened, and she'd already traversed the low-water crossings on her way there that afternoon. Conditions didn't appear to have worsened.

The next twelve hours would prove, yet again, that appearances can be deceptive.

"If I'd known what was in store for me," Sandy recalled, "I'd have turned right around and told Ellen she was going to have a houseguest for the night, like it or not." Instead, she turned the key and drove down the narrow gravel road.

Moments later, the first creek she approached looked more or less as it had several hours earlier. For most of the year, the bed was no more than a dry, sandy ribbon. Tonight, her headlight beams revealed its other, less common mood: a fast-moving, turbid, over-the-road flow. Still, Sandy judged it to be shallow enough for safe crossing. She hit the gas and pushed on, confident the vehicle had the spunk to power through.

Halfway across, her stomach lurched as she sensed everything lift off the pavement and slip sideways. Punching the accelerator, she felt tires searching for traction—without success. The car listed again, then floated free. Darkness closed in as water rose above the headlights and swept across the hood. Out the window Sandy saw water churning against the glass above the locks. Now it began to rise inside as well, quickly covering her feet and legs with an icy shock; she was wearing only a T-shirt, lightweight pants, and flip-flops.

She clung to the wheel, desperately hoping she might still pilot toward the far shore. But it spun uselessly in her hands. The engine sputtered and died, and the whole thing bumped and rocked along, now at the water's mercy.

"I started praying right then, 'Father, please stop this car!' I have no concept of time when I think back, but I know I must have repeated that at least ten times."

The car did stop—for a moment—then swung free again, this time moving backward down the creek channel. Sandy was enveloped in darkness, unable to see any surroundings. With shaking hands, she tried her phone. No service—there never was on the road between Ellen's cabin and home. "You're no good to me!" she yelled angrily, whipping it into the water, which was up to her armpits and still rising.

"Father, please stop this car, because I can't!" she prayed again.

Suddenly the vehicle came to rest facing into the current. Water still surged all around, but the Honda had caught on something, swaying side to side yet no longer headed downstream. Apart from the headlights, still submerged, Sandy could see zero light, and the sky wore a murky mask of black cloud. Houses scattered throughout the forest were few and far between, not a reasonable hope on a night like this. The car doors were locked and the power windows rolled up. She was trapped.

"I knew I could die there. The possibility felt very real—like the realization was sitting there in the car with me. I said, 'I don't want to die in this car! Not like this!'"

The instant she spoke those words aloud, the dome light flickered on. She knew immediately what it signified: the hatchback-style rear window had come open.

"On that model, the rear door swung open like a gate on a side hinge, and the rear window opened upward. It could only be opened manually from the outside—there was no release or switch inside the car. That night it popped open, and the light came on just as I cried out. I knew God had provided an exit for me."

At the time, Sandy was fifty-six and suffered from arthritis in her back and knees. The cold water had worsened matters, further stiffening her limbs and numbing her hands and feet. Even so, she scrambled over the seats in the pitch-blackness like she was twenty. She pushed open the window and climbed through into the water, still with no idea where the Honda had come to rest. Water up to her shoulders, she clung to the rear hatch, unable to touch the ground. The spare tire was mounted outside to her right, presenting an obstacle, so she moved left . . . and found solid rock just a few inches under the water's surface. She scrambled up onto a flat slab of sandstone wide enough to stand on.

"I asked God to send lightning so I could see where I was—and he did! The creek was flowing really fast, but the car looked like it had been perfectly parallel parked right next to this ledge. The forest on the bank was thick and impenetrable."

So she waited. Feeling the need to do *something*, she called out for help all night. She heard wild animals moving noisily in the nearby undergrowth; she climbed back onto the car, hoping they wouldn't decide to examine her. She worried about snakes, since water moccasins and copperheads are common in the hills. As the temperature fell and her body began to ache, she wanted desperately to lie down and sleep but knew she shouldn't. What if the water kept rising?

The rain had stopped by then, but twice, when she was about to succumb, a single icy raindrop struck the back of her neck to jolt her awake. Through the dark hours, she thought about her life and was pleasantly surprised to have no serious regrets.

Morning finally came. Sandy hoped to find a way through the woods to a nearby road or house, but it was a plan she quickly abandoned. In the growing light she realized her car had come to rest at the base of a sheer sandstone cliff. The ledge where she stood was the only footing available in any direction. The creek itself was still swollen and surging; the bank on the other side was a tangle she couldn't see beyond.

And if that weren't discouraging enough, a band of angry thunderclouds was again gathering overhead. Sandy found a way to sit down and pray.

"I knew I couldn't get out on my own and that I might be trapped there awhile. And I also knew I had nowhere to go if the water started rising again. I asked God for help and for no more rain. Just then I noticed a patch of nearby wild-flowers—brown-eyed Susans, my favorite. It felt like an answer to my prayer and a promise. The water hadn't reached those flowers the night before, so I knew it wouldn't today either."

A search had been underway for Sandy since five thirty that morning, when Gale awoke and discovered his wife was missing. Rescuers were making their way down the creek, but experience kept them from holding out much hope of finding her alive. At flood stage, those waters flowed perilously deep in places—deep enough to swallow a car.

They mostly were looking for the telltale eddies that signaled the presence of a submerged vehicle. It was hard going, too, in such rugged terrain and dense undergrowth. By nine o'clock, they had covered only three-quarters of a mile from the crossing.

"There she is!" The man's excited voice came from across the creek. Then Sandy saw his face through the trees. "Are you okay?" he yelled.

"Well, this float trip stinks!" she hollered back. "And I can't say much for the camping either!"

An hour later, after rescue workers cut a path through the forest and brought in a boat for crossing, Sandy lay safely in an ambulance. Officials told her if the car had traveled a few more feet downstream it would have entered an area where she'd likely have drowned. They praised her for doing all the right things, but she knew it had nothing to do with her. Other than losing her voice, suffering mild hypothermia, and being covered in bug bites, Sandy survived her brush with death relatively unscathed. It was God's grace, she insisted, and her mother's prayers, which she knew nothing about at the time.

Though Sandy escaped unharmed, she wasn't unchanged. "I had to go three-quarters of a mile down a creek in a flood, but I'm different now. The experience has given me a boldness I'd never had. I was always a quiet woman, yet now I'm not as afraid to tell people about God's love. When you completely and totally surrender and say, 'Father, take care of this because I can't,' that's what he's waiting to hear from us."

A Closer Look

Ever have an extremely strong impression on your heart, or the feeling that certain words are stuck in your mind? Or a sudden "awareness" that somebody you know is in trouble and you're to do something about it? Even, like Sandy's mother, a powerful and undeniable urge to pray for someone who isn't anywhere near you?

What causes these promptings? Lots of people wonder whether it's a sixth sense, an intuition, or a special-delivery message from heaven. Is it God? ESP? Nothing at all?

Most of us are familiar with a follower of Jesus named Paul. His was not a run-of-the-mill conversion story. Originally known as Saul, this devout Jewish scholar had a reputation for persecuting and arresting Christians, whom he saw as damnable heretics.

Saul was traveling near Damascus, in present-day Syria, when suddenly an inexplicably bright light shone on him. The shock of it knocked him to the ground. Adding to the moment's terror was the voice that came out of nowhere:

> "Saul, Saul, why do you persecute me?"
> "Who are you, Lord?" Saul asked.
> "I am Jesus, whom you are persecuting. . . . Now get up and go into the city, and you will be told what you must do."[1]

The blinded Saul had to depend on his companions to lead him. He stayed in Damascus three days, waiting but eating and drinking nothing. Imagine his anxiety and fear after this supernatural encounter. Later we're told he was praying during this time.[2]

Meanwhile, elsewhere in the city, a Christian named Ananias had a vision. Whether he'd been praying or simply going about his daily business, we don't know. But he was consumed with the unavoidable impression that he was to go to Straight Street, to a particular house, and ask for "a man from Tarsus named Saul."[3]

Now it was his turn to be frightened—not by a brilliant flash of light but by that name. Few men in the first century engendered more panic among believers than Saul of Tarsus. Ananias must have been thinking, *Surely, God, you know there's no way I'll go near Saul. He'd kill me!* He protested,[4] but he couldn't shake the voice that commanded, "Go! This man is my chosen instrument."[5]

Perhaps he sat for a while, gathering his courage. Maybe he wondered if this vision and the indescribable impression that had come to him were truly from God or if he were going crazy. He made his way, though, to where the notorious Saul waited.

When Saul heard Ananias was at the door, he wasn't surprised. He too had seen a vision that this man was coming to pray for him and that he, Saul, would see again.

As for Ananias, he received a warm welcome instead of being arrested and hauled off to prison. That prompting had been real: He really *was* supposed to pray for this guy.[6]

Saul converted to Christianity. His name changed to Paul, and he went on to teach, preach, become a central figure, and write a good share of the New Testament.

A Word of Knowledge

What about those impressions, hunches—visions—given to Ananias and Saul? What were they, and where did they come from? Collectively, these experiences have a name: "a word of knowledge."

In this usage, *word* can mean a single word, a phrase, or even many sentences.

More important is: *of knowledge.*

A word of knowledge consists of a strong impression on the mind—usually not an audible voice, though it could be—of something a person would not otherwise *know*. Ananias couldn't have known that Saul, who was heading to arrest Jesus' followers, had been blinded, had a change of heart, and was now awaiting him. Saul couldn't have known a man named Ananias would be coming to pray for him. *Unless* God told them. And that's what a word of knowledge is: an unusually strong impression, given by God, for a specific purpose.

Paul explains this concept in his first letter to the church in the Greek city of Corinth. God gives exceptional "gifts" or unique abilities to believers for the good of all, and one of these is "the word of knowledge."[7] Another translation calls this the gift of "special knowledge."[8]

However, the definition raises more questions. How do we *really* know such an experience is from God? What if we think it is, but it doesn't prove to be true? Is it possible, for instance, to have a strong impression we assume is from God, when its source is really an overactive imagination?

Regrettably, the answer to this last question is yes. We can be deceived by our thoughts, desires, and dreams. We need a

135

way to discern whether an impression that seems to capture our minds is truly from God.

Guidelines for a Word of Knowledge

It is vital to test any prompting that seems to direct our actions in a way that's beyond our understanding. Here are some simple guidelines:

1. *A word of knowledge will never violate biblical principles.* For example, if you think you're being urged to rob a bank, you are not hearing a message from God.
2. *A word of knowledge will always stay within God's plan.* If you're consumed by the prompting to do something immoral, God is not directing you, no matter how you may attempt to justify it.
3. *A word of knowledge will always work toward accomplishing God's will on earth.* Any time we receive a special-delivery divine message, it's intended to bring forth God's purpose for the person who received it, another person, or many other people.

Whether it's a vision, a dream, a voice, a hunch, or an unbidden thought, a word of knowledge can come in several ways.

- *Seeing it.* Again, Jesus said he only did what he saw God the Father doing.[9] Some people have said a message came to them as if they saw a newspaper headline. Prophets (like Ezekiel) and "ordinary people" (like Joseph) have been directed by God through visions.

- *Hearing it*. Jesus said he heard from the Father,[10] and this likely is the most common way to experience a word of knowledge. Although it's rarely an audible voice, it can be strong enough to seem so. For example, Joshua heard God warning him about a serious offense that turned out to be Achan's.[11]

- *Feeling or sensing it*. People sometimes report having a powerful inner sense or intuition that compels them to do something. Often, as with Sandy Rupp's mother, the urging is specifically directed, such as praying for a friend or phoning someone to check on his well-being.

- *Knowing it, without understanding why*. One fascinating biblical conversation is between Jesus and a woman in Samaria. When Jesus asked her to go get her husband, she said she didn't have one. But Jesus, "knowing" what she hadn't said, essentially replied, "That's true; though you've been married five times, you haven't married the man living with you."[12] She was stunned—how could he *know*? Yet he did. That's a word of knowledge: something we know without understanding how we could have come to know it.

- *Being "with" someone or something*. The classic example of this probably rare prompting is an account of the prophet Elisha, who knew that his servant Gehazi had lied to Naaman the Aramean, without being there when it happened. Somehow Elisha *was* there, in spirit, so that he knew what had been said.[13]

What if you have a prompting but aren't sure it's a God-given, heaven-sent message? *Ask*. Find a wise person of faith and seek guidance. Solicit a second (and third and fourth) opinion from someone whose judgment and spiritual insight you respect.

An example of this would be if an unmarried woman has the strong impression that a certain man is to be her husband, even if he's never shown interest. She may be hearing from God . . . or from her own hopes and desires. Another example would be if a person declares that this match (or job change, or move) is God's will. Allow us to make a strong recommendation: The best way to determine whether such impressions are more than someone's well-meaning imagination is to be part of a church led by a pastor who believes, understands, and teaches the Bible, including the term *word of knowledge.*

There are counterfeits to *everything* in life. Scripture warns about trying to get a "word" from a source other than God, and just as there is knowledge from him, there also are deceptions from his enemy. The devil certainly would like to deceive you, one means of which could be to give you wrong information.

For example, if you were to seek information from a deceased loved one at a séance, you would be setting yourself up to be vulnerable and misled. God states clearly that we're to seek truth from his Word and with those who are among the living.[14] Avoid anything involving extrasensory perception, Tarot cards, clairvoyance, fortune-telling, or horoscopes. These and other similar endeavors are dangerous for those who pursue them, no matter how popular or widely accepted they may be in our culture.

The earlier point bears repeating: When you've received what you think could be a God-given word of knowledge, make certain you're surrounded by people who are spiritually mature enough to help you understand whether the information can stand up to biblical principles and accomplish God's will.

The Purpose Behind Special Messages

Why would someone receive an authentic word of knowledge? Because God loves his people, and there are times when he wants them to know something that can't be known by human means. The answer is no less and no more than this.

Think of it this way: Both of us, the authors, are dads. As we've worked, we have stopped writing many times and talked with our children. Why? Because we love them. There have been recent moments when communicating with them was a top (sometimes *the* top) priority.

So it is with God. Communicating with us is important to him, and sometimes he wants to give his kids specific information for a specific purpose. When he does, we're sometimes more prone to give it a fancy label than we are to seeking earnestly to confirm and follow it.

Don't be alarmed by such messages. In fact, be grateful for them, for they show that he loves us and others in our lives so much that he wants to make sure we know what we need to know. His powerful promptings in this way are another means by which heaven touches earth.

10

THE DANCING HAND OF GOD

CAN PRAYER PRODUCE A MIRACLE?

Brain tumor. It's hard to imagine two more terrifying words.

They were uttered to Derek and Marie Packard by her neurologist on September 22, 1998. After moments of shock and several stammered questions, the couple stood outside his office, held each other tightly, and cried together. Despite their strong belief in God, they felt thrown into a sudden abyss of uncertainty and dread.

Marie had just received news no one wants.

Prior to the daunting diagnosis, their lives had been smooth sailing. They lived by picturesque Lake Tahoe. Derek's video production company was thriving, while Marie thrived on raising their two young daughters, Bailey and Holly. The family was involved in a church pastored by Marie's dad. Life had been joyful and predictable.

Little did they know, their brain-tumor crisis had begun the previous year. Marie had finished nursing Holly when she noticed her menstrual cycle hadn't resumed, even after many months. She mentioned this to her OB/GYN, who used medication to attempt kick-starting her cycle. After this failed, the doctor theorized that Marie may have begun early menopause.

"That seemed awfully early," recalled Marie, then in her mid-thirties. "But it had happened to my mom, so we figured that was a possibility."

Around the same time, she noticed another peculiarity: when she turned her head to look—say, when glancing backward to change lanes on the highway—there was a lag until her eyes caught up, and her right eye plainly wasn't tracking like it should. During a visit, her mother, Marilyn, likewise had observed Marie's eyes not moving in unison.

After a series of optometrist and neurologist appointments, plus subsequent scans and tests, the doctors concluded that a brain tumor behind Marie's left eye had wrapped around the optical nerve and filled her pituitary gland. This also was the reason she hadn't ovulated for the previous two years.

Marilyn remembered their post-diagnosis shock: "When the MRI came back, we all felt like we'd been punched in the gut. Bewilderment. Anguish. We couldn't believe this was happening to our 'little girl.'"

By now the Packards were in the process of relocating to Sacramento. And many more changes were hurtling toward them. As anyone knows who's ever experienced a life-threatening illness, a whirlwind of tests, treatments, and appointments consumes patient *and* caregivers.

Prayer was a constant respite and source of strength throughout their years-long ordeal. Derek and Marie enlisted the prayers of friends, families, fellow church members, and even strangers across the country. Parishioners from their home church of Trinity Life Center prayed continually. A friend, Pastor Francis Anfuso at The Rock of Roseville church, conducted a special service for them. Several similar gatherings carried Derek and Marie on a wave of hope and faith in God.

Both extended families rallied around and helped determine the best course of action. They chose a highly reputable surgeon at the UC San Francisco Medical Center, and brain surgery was scheduled. The physician told Derek and Marie that he would only remove a small portion of the tumor in order to relieve pressure; trying to do more was too dangerous and likely would blind Marie. Though he could take out only a fragment, the surgeon had great news: The tumor was a benign (noncancerous) meningioma, slow-growing and possibly eradicable through radiation.

Post-surgery and recovery, the family again relocated, now to Los Angeles for a round of intensive radiation. A new localized procedure called Steriotactic Radiotherapy, pioneered at UCLA, was performed twice daily for eight weeks. After more than a hundred treatments, the physician announced that the tumor tissue would no longer grow.

There was bad news too, however. The doctor confirmed that Marie wouldn't be able to have more children, since her pituitary was still full of the tissue and had been heavily radiated. This came as a serious blow; the couple had always dreamed of a large family. Derek especially had anticipated raising a son, or two, or three, and that dream seemed to have vanished.

143

Derek asked the physician bluntly, "Are you telling us that having another child would be a miracle?"

"Absolutely," the doctor said. "It would be a miracle if she ever conceived again."

Derek remembers vividly thinking, *The medical community has had its last word on this issue. Now we'll see what God can do.*

The prognosis proved true, as Marie soon went into menopause. Over the next several months, the couple dealt with all the hormonal ups and downs that accompany this emotional and physiological transition.

During that season, there was no evidence of a miracle. But they maintained hope in Marie's ability to achieve full recovery. They both felt God telling them that Marie would be healed gradually and not immediately. What's more, they believed they'd have another child.

"We never lost faith that God could do the impossible," Marie added.

———— ❧ ————

In 2001, Derek and Marie felt led to move to Colorado Springs. Thereafter they felt urged to pray for another child, though Marie hadn't ovulated for nearly seven years.

In 2002, the couple was introduced to the "Temple Prayer," a method developed by South Korea's David Yonggi Cho, pastor of the world's largest church. It's based on the worship process of the Old Testament tabernacle, regarded by the Israelites as the most sacred of places.[1] Derek began devoting himself to this prayer, which typically lasts an hour. In time, Marie noticed significant changes in her husband: more joy, patience, and optimism. She soon decided to join him in this approach.

They prayed the Prayer together each morning for eight months. As time went on, Marie experienced inner healing from emotional issues she'd wrestled with for decades.

———— ✆ ————

At a 2003 Sunday night service in New Life Church, the Packards' home congregation, special speaker David Hogan held a prayer time afterward for anyone who needed healing. Bailey, ten, said, "Mom, you should go to the front and be prayed for!"

Marie resisted but went forward to honor her daughter's urging and faith. Bailey walked beside her mother, nudging her down the aisle.

Hogan then prayed for Marie and others, and nothing dramatic happened. Even so, in his simple prayer for courage and strength, Bailey felt something. "Mom," she said with conviction, "you're healed. It is definitely done."

———— ✆ ————

One Friday in late summer 2004, a good friend came over for dinner, and the conversation turned to adopting children. Since Derek and Marie had longed for a big, bustling brood, they increasingly began to consider this as an option, wondering if adoption might be how God wanted to expand their family.

The very next night, Derek and Marie were in bed, debriefing about the day, when she felt something strange near her abdomen. "That's weird," she said, and placed Derek's hand on her stomach. He felt an undeniable tap, tap, tap.

"Right out of the movie *Alien,*" he joked. "Definitely, something was in there!"

Their minds began to race. Overwhelmed by the possibilities, Derek rushed to the nearest Walgreens and purchased a pregnancy test. Three, actually. And, back at home, all three showed the distinctive blue line: *Positive*. Marie stood, stunned, "like a deer in the headlights," while her family danced wildly around the house.

At the OB/GYN's office a few days later, the sonogram showed a six-month-old fetus growing inside Marie. Not only that, the images indicated a boy.

Derek and Marie wondered: How could she be six months along when she hadn't seemingly put on any weight or shown any other telltale signs? What's more, she'd been forced to wear a leg cast for four months after breaking several bones in a fall. The cast had made sexual intimacy almost impossible; in fact, they'd had relations only *once*. When they revealed this to their pastor, he called it "a miraculous conception."

On December 15, 2004, their son DJ—the one doctors said would never be born—came into the world with no complications or physical problems.

"Every time we look at DJ, we think of God's faithfulness and marvel at his power," Derek said. He notes four factors that combined to convince them it was a miracle: Marie suddenly resumed a normal menstrual cycle after ten years; she had already gone through menopause; the physicians were adamant she would never conceive again; they had only a single intimate episode at the time DJ was conceived.

Just to make sure the Packards and all their friends knew God was at work, another son, Johndavid, arrived in 2007. God's grace was the gift that kept on giving.

Derek concluded, "I have no doubt it was prayer—ours as a couple and the hundreds of people praying for us—that not only saw Marie through a brain tumor but also produced two sons."

A Closer Look

We've defined miracles as events that transcend our present scientific understanding. In addition, many think of miracles as public displays or manifestations of divine power. Derek and Marie, with a household full of rambunctious kids, certainly agree. One related question, then: Is there anything we, as recipients of miracles, can do to bring them about? Or are they happenings that we can't influence through any means?

We can get to an answer by way of linguistics. In the Bible, the words translated *manifest* and *manifestation* describe times when God is revealed or at work in unique ways. *Manifest* is from two Latin terms: *manus,* which means "hand" and is the root of "manual" and "manicure," and *festum,* which refers to a holiday, festival, or celebration. Thus, a *divine manifestation* might be rendered as "the dancing hand of God."

One significant aspect of this expression is the apparent randomness of divine manifestation. A miracle may seem to us like a "dancing hand" that appears unexpectedly and behaves unpredictably. Think of the way a dancer might spin and point and extend as he leaps around. While any specific contact point on the floor could appear to the audience to be random, his steps are choreographed precisely, and there is an overarching pattern and purpose to the routine.

147

One scriptural statement in particular provides further insight. The apostle Paul says the Holy Spirit's manifestation *"is given."*[2] If those two words alone don't seem very important, consider their significance.

First, the verb *is* is in the present tense, signifying action that's continuous, ongoing. In other words, rather than relegating them to the past, we can expect miraculous manifestations to keep happening.

Second, the verb's voice is passive, meaning we're recipients of God's "dancing hand." If Paul wanted to say that we alone initiate miracles, he would have used the active voice. If he'd intended to demonstrate that we help miracles to happen alongside or together with God's power, he would have utilized the middle voice. He didn't need either of these—he used the passive because that's the answer.

Miracles are gifts from God and not something "worked up" by us. We don't make miracles happen—we receive them.

Doing Our Part?

But if you think this means there's no way in which we might "prompt" God, hold on. It isn't enough to note the apparent randomness of supernatural events and to say we don't produce them. We need to delve a bit deeper into the reality of the metaphysical.

Regardless of popular usage, miracles are *not* merely "anything unusual or not readily explainable," like scoring front-row theatre seats or rush-hour traffic clearing up at the exact moment needed for racing to an appointment. They're a divine means to show humans the realm beyond the physical. In that sense, a miracle is about revealing God, not entertaining us or making our lives easier (although those are two possible outcomes).

Still, lots of people think miracles are mechanistic: If they're ultimately "from God," he watches from a distance and, aloof from the created order, doesn't interfere. As such, miracles are an aberration of the natural world but still are attributable to nature.

That's false. Miracles aren't inevitable movements of an impersonal reality. If they were, we wouldn't label them "miracles" anyway—we'd say, "The natural world sometimes functions this way."

Another popular myth says that not only can we cause the miraculous, but we also can design its effect. One recent example is Rhonda Byrne's bestseller *The Secret,* in which she teaches that if you emit good thoughts into the "universe," then they'll bounce back and deliver what you want. A sympathetic website explains it like this: "We create our lives, with every thought every minute of every day. Living The Secret offers tools and ideas to help you live The Secret and create the life of your dreams."[3]

According to this theory, if you send out the right thoughts in the right way for long enough, you should be able to walk to the mailbox and find not bills but only checks. Transmit the "fact" that you're ready for triathlons and you'll get slim, trim, and lithe. In other words, *you* produce miracles.[4]

We don't believe miracles are a consequence of the natural order or that our thought processes can activate them (although later we'll discuss the role of biblically founded faith). Miracles flow directly from God, at his will and for his reasons. They're neither random coincidental events nor self-generated wish-fulfillments. God, the source and author of all miracles, performs them as he chooses in order to establish his purpose and reveal his character.

The all-loving, all-powerful God decides when and how to touch his people with his "dancing hand." In other words, *miracles are relationally based.* They flow from an existing relationship between God and a person or from a relationship God desires to have with a person.

Seeking What We Need

A relationally based understanding of miracles suggests that, although God's hand never can be forced by human will, what we do in our relationship with him makes a difference. Humans *don't* produce miracles, generate supernatural events, or compel God to intervene. However, one substantial way we can contribute is by praying in faith.

Faith-filled prayer has an impact. While some miracles are entirely unanticipated, most are prayed for, believed for, and— yes—even expected. God hears and responds to the cries and requests of his children. For instance, there seems to be a significant correlation between prayer and healing. Although God's answer isn't always yes, the times when miraculous healing comes are evidence of his love for us.

We aren't talking about some kind of "attraction" we can create for miracles, as in *The Secret,* or in Byrne's subsequent book, *The Power,* in which she claims, "You will come to understand that all it takes is just one thing to change your relationships, money, health, happiness, career, and your entire life. . . . The life of your dreams has always been closer to you than you realized, because *The Power*—to have everything good in your life—is inside you."[5] In contrast, the correct attitude isn't to be "Look what I can do" but rather "Look what God has done!"

Within the terms of our discussion, there are two types of prayer: petitionary (asking) and declarative (affirming).

- A petitionary prayer says, "God, help me. Please do this. Amen."

- A declarative prayer says, "God, I know you're my loving Father and desire to help me. Knowing you've given me authority to speak your will on earth, I proclaim your will over this situation. Since all good things come from you, I thank you in advance that either I'll receive the miracle needed this moment or I'll experience the miracle of soaring above what I now face. Amen."

God hears and answers both types. The first prayer isn't the wrong way to pray. In many desperate or dangerous situations, it's a natural first response. In those times, we're like little children crying out to Daddy.

The second prayer, however, might be more effective because it more fully takes into account the design of prayer itself. The first one has an element that might be likened to begging. The second one demonstrates confidence and strength in understanding that God has given his children authority not only to come to him with requests but also to stand down the opposition in the king's name. It's as if God has said, "I want the best for you, and you're in a very broken world. I give you authority to declare those things you know to be my will so you needn't think you must implore me to act. Face what you must overcome with the assurance that I'm backing up your declaration."

Bold declarative prayer is what Jesus modeled for his followers. In Matthew's gospel he instructs through what we call the Lord's Prayer (or better rendered, the Lord's example of how we should pray). Regarding the pattern, we're directed to pray for his will to be done *on earth, as in heaven.* His will always is for our ultimate good.

Either Way, We Pray

Good fathers want to be loving and kind to their children. We desire great things for our kids, although at times we must say no to their requests. However we respond to them and relate to them, we want it to be for their ultimate good. God, the perfect father, most assuredly wants the best things for us, which means at times he too must say no.

God is delighted when we, based on the authority he's given us, face life's difficulties and dangers with declarations of victory over them: "Your kingdom come! Your will be done on earth!" What's the comparison? "As in heaven." And things in heaven are *awesome.* Simply awesome!

Granted, our circumstances in this broken-down world can never be as trouble-free as our promised future eternity. But through faith-filled prayers, God seems to give us glimpses of that guarantee through his mercy and grace in answering our petitions and providing miracles.

Can you do anything to bring about a miracle? The answer: God is God, we're not. But for reasons unknown, just as God willingly relates with us, so also he partners with us. He makes miracles happen; through our prayers we can see them happen.

Additionally, you can create a climate in which God's Spirit actively is invited to move. Following the pattern of prayer Jesus provides tends to create the atmosphere of expectancy that opens doors and invites God in to work the miraculous.

11

Back From the Dead

THE PENULTIMATE MIRACLE:
DYING AND RETURNING TO LIFE

O f all the miracles ever recorded, the ones that seem most incredible are those that include someone once dead coming back to life.

Christians, every Easter Sunday, affirm that this has happened, celebrating the resurrection of Jesus. And we accept the biblical accounts of Lazarus and others.

Even so, somehow the leap from then to now can seem a bit too much. A person actually dying and then returning . . . *today?* People of deep faith themselves harbor skepticism about such "tales."

The story of Milton Green has fascinated me (Jim) for decades. I'd assumed it was true—at least I'd thought it was. But I had nagging back-of-the-mind doubts: What if I hadn't heard it right? What if my memory was fuzzy? What if it never really happened?

Concerned that wishful thinking had outdistanced reality, I called my friend Jesse McElreath, an eyewitness. "What happened that day when Milton Green died?" I asked. Jesse then recounted in vivid detail his astounding experience in Lake Country Estates, a beautiful upscale community north of Fort Worth.

⸺ ❧ ⸺

Allow me to introduce Milton Green, who referred to himself as "a Baptist carpet cleaner from Cleveland, Tennessee." One day he began to read the Bible. Not like most of us read it, a few verses at a time. He read it for eight hours a day. He did this for years.

By the time he moved to the Dallas–Fort Worth area, Green had an unbelievable command of Scripture. He believed God's Word was the source of all truth and power.

In the early 1980s he began teaching a three-day "In the Word" seminar that didn't feature any conventional preaching. This unschooled, distinctly southern, blue-collar man uniquely and persuasively strung verses together.

By the time I attended, several thousand were flocking to his sessions, which required moving to the Dallas Convention Center Theatre. The might and authority of the Scriptures resonated throughout the entire place as he prayed the seminar-closing prayer. This prayer itself often lasted an hour or more.

How could a rough-hewn carpet cleaner pack out auditoriums with eager listeners, including many pastors? The answer for me is that Milton Green laid out biblical truth in a way that utterly gripped our hearts.

But then, one spring day, Milton Green died.

This is where a pastor at Lake Country Baptist Church, Jesse McElreath, enters. Jesse had received an urgent call: "Come quickly! Milt had a heart attack."

He arrived at the Green home to find emergency personnel already there. Green lay on the floor with one leg up on the bed, in and out of consciousness, with sporadic breathing. Each time he came to, he refused to let a paramedic even touch him. He absolutely refused to receive oxygen or any other assistance. "Just pray over me and speak God's Word over me," he'd say, then go out again.

One medic with extensive training said the EMTs could not merely stand by without taking action. The team then asked Jesse to sign a medical release form indicating they weren't liable for being denied permission to help a now pulseless man.

Friends who had gathered prayed over Green's body as the ambulance crew helplessly watched. Jesse wondered if he were doing the right thing by honoring his friend's stalwart insistence. After some hesitation, he reluctantly signed the release form, sending away the EMTs, Green's last, best hope for human help.

One friend, Bev, who was medically trained, began to pray over Green's arteries and veins—tracing them, as it were.

Green, who appeared to have suffered a heart attack, was dead, with no pulse.

The house had a large sliding glass door. Neighbors, alarmed by the presence of so many cars and an ambulance, were peering through it into the confusion. "The scene was amazing," Jesse said. "Some twenty-five to thirty people came and went during the three-hour ordeal."

He describes those awful moments conclusively: "There was no life in Milton."

Remarkably, the one person who seemed unconcerned was Green's wife, Joyce. She loved her husband greatly but was as faith-filled as he; she believed that if God's healing words were prayed over him, he'd be fine. In fact, she was so convinced of this that she went to her bedroom and took her time as she showered, fixed her hair and dressed, then calmly reemerged amid the chaotic roomful of anxious people praying.

Green would later report that during this time, he "saw the Holy Spirit, and he told me, 'Don't leave your body.'"

As prayer continued, he suddenly began to show signs of life. After a while, he even appeared somewhat *normal.* At strong urging, he consented to go with Dr. Ernest Byers to Harris Hospital in Fort Worth to at least learn what had taken place.

Tests confirmed that he'd suffered a heart attack. How he survived was unknown. Green returned home that evening and enjoyed a meal, though he remained in bed.

After his death and return to life, he went on to live another fifteen years.

I was with Jesse McElreath a short time after this event. He too was amazed and perplexed. The details he related that day are exactly as he recalled them more than twenty-five years later.

This is one of the few "rising from the dead" accounts where I know and can personally vouch for the persons involved. I've heard others, and I believe some to be true. But this is one in which I actually knew the eyewitnesses.

Can we medically verify that Milton Green was truly dead? The emergency personnel left, so no, we can't. However, he had no pulse for some time, and the one person present who had a medically related vocation regarded him as absolutely, certainly dead.[1] Furthermore, while I don't mean to discredit episodes that happen more quickly, we're not talking about a few minutes—again, this incident lasted hours.

Recalling what occurred that day, I've also pondered what Green himself said later: "I knew that Satan would try to take me out. I knew that if they'd just pray the Word of God over me, I would be fine."

Stories like Milton Green's are plentiful, both in our own time and in times gone by. We've noted that some of the most remarkable accounts in modern times come from the life of the Englishman Smith Wigglesworth. He is said to have raised at least fourteen people from the dead, including one woman who—having briefly enjoyed heaven's bliss—slapped him in the face for bringing her back.

In that vein, probably topping the "humor file" list is the man brought on a stretcher, directly from the hospital, to a public service. When he was healed after Wigglesworth prayed over him, he jumped up and moved excitedly about, oblivious to how his gaping hospital gown was revealing his entire backside.[2]

Wigglesworth was one in a long line of individuals known for raising people from the dead. There are many accounts of resuscitations either performed or experienced by such men and women as Saint Anastasius, Saint Patrick, Saint Julian of Antioch, Saint Archelides, Saint Joan of Arc, Saint Francis of Paola, Saint Winifred (raised to life by the prayers of her uncle, Saint Beuno), Saint Stanislaus of Krakow. That an entire book would be titled *Saints Who Raised the Dead: True Stories of 400 Resurrection Miracles* is an indication that resuscitations are not altogether infrequent.[3]

Resuscitation vs. Resurrection

When we say "raised from the dead," in this sense, do we mean a resurrection? Actually, a person being clinically dead (from drowning, for instance) and then being brought back to life isn't the same thing. Fantastic as it might be, this is resuscitation, not resurrection.

Resuscitation is a temporary revival of this mortal life, as in the account of Milton Green, who later died (again). Sometimes resuscitation is accomplished through purely medical means, as when a heart has stopped and is restarted by doctors. Other times, resuscitation is made possible only through a miracle—not the same miracle as resurrection, but a miracle nonetheless. Elisha the prophet participated in a miraculous resuscitation when he brought a Shunammite's son back to life.[4] Jesus performed a similar miracle for Jairus, the synagogue leader, by restoring his daughter.[5] It's well known that Jesus brought his friend Lazarus back from the dead, also a clear example of resuscitation.[6]

Resurrection is a permanent phenomenon. While people who are resuscitated, or "raised," come back to life but die once more at some later time, to be resurrected means never to die again.

The Bible's use of the word *resurrection* refers to a time when we will transfer from mortality (being subject to death) to immortality (not being subject to death). Remember, God did not intend people to die; he created us immortal and perfect, physically and spiritually. He designed us to live forever. Our first ancestors, Adam and Eve, damaged that design when they turned away from God and bought into Satan's deception to join his rebellion. Satan cannot create but can only destroy—he brought the corruptions of mortality and death.

Fortunately, God is merciful, and because of the salvation he has made available, we have been granted a path back to eternal life. We'll enjoy immortality in heaven, which isn't some cosmic graveyard where people go when they die because they have to go *somewhere*. Heaven, rather, is a continuation of life. One day, we'll be resurrected.

We don't know everything about our future glorified, resurrected bodies, but we believe they likely will be similar to the body Jesus had after he rose from the dead.[7] If that's the case, we can make some assumptions.[8]

After being resurrected, Jesus was immortal and ready for heaven. He was recognizable to those around him but also did things no ordinary person could do, like miraculously travel through locked doors and appear before his disciples to confront Thomas.[9] The coming kingdom briefly broke into the present reality, which gives us an intriguing glimpse of our future.

Further, in our resurrected bodies we'll no longer have a "sin nature," a built-in bent toward wrongdoing. Instead we'll be like Adam *before* he fell, for though he chose to reject God he was born sinless.[10] The afterlife, then, really is a reestablishment and continuation of the life God intended from the start.

Death Is Not Final

Jesus wept when he arrived at the home of the deceased Lazarus. He didn't weep because death is final—he more than anyone was aware of eternal life's reality and he knew he'd be restoring his friend to life within moments. Yet still he cried, and for good reason: Humans were never meant to die. Death means that something has been broken; something isn't right. Death is a tragedy despite the hope of the coming resurrection. Jesus did what we do when our good friends die: He felt sorrow and grief.

In addition to its demonstration of Christ's love and compassion, there are other lessons in this account.

LAZARUS LESSON #1

At the very time Jesus was raising Lazarus, religious leaders in Jerusalem were plotting to eliminate him. Jesus had traveled to Bethany, only two miles east. There, almost in the presence of those who meant to kill him, he raised a man from the grave.

See the irony—the juxtaposition of life and death? The man they thought they could kill raised another to rejoin the living. You would think the arrogant elite might have said, "How can we destroy *him*—he brings dead people back to life!"

But they didn't get it, even though he gave them a big clue. Speaking about his own resurrection, Jesus would demonstrate the truth of his words by raising Lazarus: "I am the resurrection and the life. The one who believes in me will . . . never die. Do you believe this?"[11] The miracle was his not-so-subtle way of saying, "You can't destroy me; I give life. I *am* life, and here's the proof: 'Lazarus, come out!'"[12]

LAZARUS LESSON #2

Through the raising of Lazarus, Jesus gave a prophecy. A prophet's words must be validated in order for people to know he's not a charlatan, and God hasn't always compelled people to wait before delivering an obvious verdict as to the prophet's credibility. For this purpose, a long-range prediction often has been preceded by a short-range prediction and fulfillment. Miracles can serve as a dynamic verification, and as with many of his other works, the return of Lazarus validated Jesus' earthly life and role.

LAZARUS LESSON #3

There's more. Through the Lazarus experience, Jesus brought another "time zone" into ours and let discerning people see into the future. Again, he invited the coming kingdom (the way things will be) to break into this present era (the way things currently are) so we could glimpse how it will be when death no longer has any power. Lazarus's temporary return foreshadowed a day of permanence when life forever will reign.

Jesus, speaking of the ultimate resurrection of human beings, gave a sneak preview by raising Lazarus at his friend's own funeral. The raising (even in a mortal state) served as a kind of down payment on a guaranteed and eagerly awaited event. The resuscitations Jesus did were small-measure appetizers to the upcoming main course.

Normally we're limited by our understanding and perspective to this earth as it is now. Jesus wanted us to see beyond, and to aid our vision he performed works to bring the next and final age into the now so that, for a moment, we'd see life as it will be: without any heartache, sickness, suffering, or death. And there are some who've already tasted it for themselves.

We began this chapter by telling about Milton Green, whose amazing raised-from-the-dead story was only slightly questionable because no medical staff "officially" declared him deceased. We'll finish this discussion with a more recent account of a patient whose death was verified by two physicians and other medical personnel. If you wonder whether dead-and-alive miracles still happen, read on.

Modern-Day Miracle: Praying a Patient Back to Life

"Dr. Crandall, please report to the ER. Dr. Crandall to the ER."
To Chauncey Crandall, the voice coming through the hospital sound system on Wednesday morning, September 20, 2006, was like nails on a chalkboard.

His shift as the on-duty cardiologist at the Palm Beach Cardiovascular Clinic in Florida had barely begun, and already he was swamped while making his rounds in the ICU. Thirty minutes earlier he'd heard the previous announcement, about the victim of a severe heart attack arriving, but he'd hoped the ER staff could handle the situation.

Harried, and now a little irritated, he set off to see just how substantially his completely packed morning was about to be disrupted.

It was like walking into a war zone. The room was engulfed in a frantic battle to resuscitate fifty-three-year-old Jeff Markin. For forty minutes they had tried everything to restart his heart. Among other techniques, they'd used electric shock at least a dozen times, without effect. The staff needed Crandall not to assist with the intervention but to confirm the decision to end the effort and declare Markin dead. After evaluating everything done already, Crandall agreed—there was nothing more to attempt.

"There was no life left in him," Crandall said. "He was literally black with death. His face and hands and feet were already cyanotic from lack of blood flow and oxygen."

While one nurse remained in the room, preparing Markin's body for removal to the morgue, Crandall completed the necessary paperwork. Then, eager to resume his rounds, he headed back toward the ICU.

"On the way I heard this voice say, *'Turn around and pray for that man.'* And I wanted to argue with that voice, because I said to myself, *How can I pray for him—he's dead, he's gone, there's no life in him.*"

So he ignored what he'd heard and kept walking. Until the voice returned: *"Turn around and go pray for that man."*

The physician stopped to consider the prompting he now knew was from God. A devout Christian, he was a firm believer in divine intervention and the power of prayer. Still, he paused. He could afford no pointless delays. Furthermore, praying with living patients is one thing—but to pray over a corpse? What would the staff make of that?

Despite his reservations, Crandall did turn around. The nurse tending to Markin's body was puzzled and a little alarmed when the doctor reappeared at the bedside.

"I stood there, the nurse wanting to know what I was doing, and I prayed, 'Father God, I cry out to you for this man's soul. If he doesn't know you as his Lord and Savior, raise him from the dead right now in Jesus' name.'"

Just then the on-duty ER doctor entered the room and also was startled to see his colleague. Crandall astonished him further with an unorthodox request: one last electric shock.

Naturally, he refused; the patient had lacked a heartbeat for more than forty minutes and already was declared dead—on Crandall's authority, no less. To shock again was well off the map of approved professional procedure.

"I asked him to do it for me, personally," Crandall said. "Out of respect and honor for me, he changed his mind and did it." The stunned nurse looked on as the defibrillator paddles on Markin's discolored chest sent one last charge through his body.

"Immediately his heartbeat came back. It was instantaneous—perfect and regular, which hadn't happened at any time when the staff worked so hard to revive him. The nurse screamed, 'What have you done?'"

Markin breathed his first since collapsing in the waiting room, and he moved his hands. The ER re-erupted in frenzied activity as they whisked him away to the ICU.

That morning Jeff Markin had gotten in his car and headed to work like always. Something was wrong, though, and he knew it. He called his boss and reported not feeling well; his boss was alarmed by his symptoms and persuaded him to go to the ER.

Markin recalls that conversation but not what happened next. He can't remember driving to the hospital and has no recollection of collapsing there. He knows nothing of the ensuing battle to save his life or of Dr. Crandall's prayer.

An unbeliever at the time, he does remember lying in a coffin in a dark, deserted room for what felt an eternity. Unable to move, he was intensely disappointed that no one—friends, co-workers, family members—had come to see him, and he felt abandoned and alone. Finally, after a seemingly vast wait, a group of men arrived to wrap up his body and throw him in the "trash." It was a horrifying and hellish experience.

After three days of unconsciousness, Markin woke up— with no discernable damage to his brain or his heart. Apart from temporary numbness in his hands and feet, there was no evidence to suggest he'd ever suffered a fatal heart attack. He'd returned from death in perfect health.

—⁂—

The following Monday, Crandall visited Markin in his hospital room. Hearing about the man's despairing near-death experience, he suggested praying again—for salvation.

"He asked me at that time if I was willing to accept God into my life and into my heart," Markin said. "I just opened my arms and accepted God. It was a very emotional time. I remember just crying in his arms."

The encounter was transforming for Crandall as well: "That day when I prayed for God to raise him from the dead was a day of very little faith for me. It wasn't one of my big 'God days.' To tell the truth, when I walked into that emergency room I didn't want to stay and pray, because I was so much in a rush with my work. But I did pray. I didn't have a lot of faith backing that prayer up, but the Lord asked me to do it so I honored him and prayed. That's all we need, just a little spark of faith like that mustard seed. Miracles are real, and they are real today."[13]

12

HEAVEN'S SPECIAL FORCES

WHEN GOD SENDS HIS ANGELS
TO INTERVENE

Leroy Lane and his family had recently moved to Arizona so he could recover from the allergies that had plagued him in their native Michigan. On a hot and bright Saturday in May 1981, he'd decided to take them on an exploration of the country surrounding their new home. Maybe they would see new sights out here, east of Phoenix.

For a self-described flatlander, though, navigating a big blue Chevy van above fifteen hundred feet on a narrow, rock-strewn mountain road was nerve-wracking. Leroy focused hard on every switchback. Just twelve inches past the asphalt's edge, sometimes on both sides, the road fell away sharply and steeply to deep canyons. Leroy's discomfort was palpable as they climbed and climbed.

Still, they were so close to the sky he almost felt he could reach out and shake hands with God.

Up ahead was a small metal sign pointing left: MORMON FLAT DAM.

He took the turn.

"What are we doing?" asked his wife, Fran.

"Going to see Mormon Flat Dam," Leroy answered. "It's an adventure!"

Football-sized rocks littered the way and impeded their progress on one of the roughest tracks Leroy had ever seen. He slowed to a crawl, but the van still caromed and banked around like a pinball.

Finally they reached a small flat area—maybe fifty feet long, fifteen feet wide—that marked the trail's end. Sheer rock walls bordered this minuscule "parking lot" to the right and straight ahead. To the left was a narrow ramp that dropped to another flat area twenty-five feet below. On both sides of the ramp and beyond the lower flat area was a drop-off of hundreds of feet.

Disembarking to look around, the Lanes discovered another couple in a station wagon on the lower level. They heard rushing water, but there was no sign of the dam.

"Must have missed a turnoff someplace," Leroy surmised. There was no path, nothing to indicate a landmark. He had to admit defeat. "Okay," he conceded. "Let's get back in the van."

Leroy realized the tiny "lot" didn't offer enough room to turn around the van. But he could see the ramp in his rearview mirror. If he could back down a few feet, the ramp would provide just enough space to get the van pointed back toward the way out.

After turning the wheel, he inched the Chevy back. He felt the rear wheels descend. But he still needed more room to complete the turn. He inched backed more.

Suddenly, the van's front left corner slumped.

Uh-oh.

He lowered his window and peered down.

The left front tire dangled over open space. Leroy gingerly cracked open the door to make sure he wasn't hallucinating. Sure enough, the view went down and down and down. Instantly the Lanes were in a dangerously precarious predicament.

"Everybody stay calm," he warned—as much for himself as for his family.

His heart sank as he pondered: They were more than fifty miles from home on a nearly deserted mountain. His Chevy now blocked the wagon below. There was no emergency call box, and this was long before cell phones. No chance of calling for help.

No doubt about it: They were in big trouble.

"Everybody out on the right," he said with quiet firmness. "Get clear of the van."

They quickly obeyed.

Leroy hadn't been wearing his seatbelt. Now he strapped it on and cautiously straightened his wheels. He shifted into drive and attempted to inch forward.

The Chevy had rear-wheel drive, and the back wheels couldn't find traction on the slippery stone. They were stuck.

He climbed out the right passenger door for a closer look. Fran and the couple from the station wagon now joined him.

Leroy shook his head. "How are we going to get this thing out of here?"

"Well, we could push," the other man offered. "We can help you."

"Thanks—I guess it's worth a try."

Leroy crawled back across and into his seat. The three other adults took positions at the van's back. Leroy tapped the accelerator, yet on every attempt the tires just spun.

"I think you need to give it more gas!" the man called.

"I think you're right, we need more horsepower!"

The Lanes' sons stepped up as well. Leroy floored it when the five of them were ready, but he stopped when he heard a *thud*.

Wondering what had happened, he scrambled across and out again. Everyone was gathered around Fran, who was gritting her teeth and examining her leg. Leroy saw a large area on her thigh quickly growing black and blue. The spinning right rear tire had found just enough traction to grab a huge stone and hurl it toward his wife.

"Fran, I am so sorry." He felt terrible. He also was more worried than ever. Fran was able to stand but was clearly in pain. Her leg didn't seem broken, but what if her injury was more serious than it appeared? How were they going to get medical attention?

Their adventure was turning into a nightmare.

Leroy didn't know what to do, but he didn't want his family to know that. Going back to the driver's seat as if he had a plan, he closed his eyes and bowed his head. "Lord," he prayed aloud, "*I need your help now!*"

When he opened his eyes, he was stunned to see an old Buick LeSabre come within a few feet of the van's front bumper and then stop.

The front doors opened, and out stepped two characters Leroy would've avoided on any other occasion. They were big men, with unshaven faces and dark, scruffy hair to their shoulders. Both wore blue jeans, sleeveless T-shirts, and red bandannas. They looked like they belonged on Harleys.

"You guys need help," the driver said. It was a statement, not a question.

Leroy wasn't sure he trusted them. Their expressions weren't menacing, but they weren't smiling either. Their look was businesslike—they were there to do a job.

No matter their intentions, Leroy couldn't deny the dire circumstances. "We certainly do."

One positioned himself at the front of the van on Leroy's side while the other moved to its rear.

"Turn your wheel to the right," the first instructed.

That didn't make sense to Leroy. But even as he doubted, he felt a sense of calm and assurance wash over him. He somehow understood that these men knew what they were doing and would help.

"Okay, back down slowly. Easy now."

Leroy did as he was told.

"Brake!" called the second man a moment later.

For the next few minutes, the men gave instructions on how to maneuver. They spoke in quiet confidence, never contradicting each other. Leroy had the sense they'd done this many times.

Soon, Leroy had all four wheels on the ramp and was backing down to the lower flat area. Finally on level ground, he instantly turned his head back to make sure all the others were safe and accounted for.

A second later, he turned his head forward again. He wanted to thank the two men who'd helped them—maybe even saved them.

But the men were gone.

Leroy blinked. *Where did those guys go? How'd they do that?*

His mind raced. They'd been standing close to the van. Even if they'd somehow scampered up the ramp and out of sight in the moment he turned his head, where was the Buick? Turning it around would have required the same maneuvering down the ramp that Leroy had just completed. Even if they'd backed out as they came in—which would have been foolhardy—through his open window Leroy would have heard them on the rocks.

He ran up the ramp, his eyes scanning everywhere for clues, but there were none. The men and the LeSabre had vanished.

Leroy returned to his family. No one had seen the men leave. It was a mystery . . . yet not to Leroy. While he'd never knowingly seen angels before, there was no other explanation. And hadn't they appeared the moment after his prayer?

God sent them. He sent helpers at just the right moment to keep us from harm. I have just witnessed heaven's angels coming to the rescue of human beings.

Leroy's planned outing, which had come so close to disaster, had turned into an adventure of faith.

"Thank you, Lord," he said aloud. "Thank you. Thank you. Thank you."

Leroy has talked about what happened at Mormon Flat Dam many times since. "Some people, after I tell the story, still doubt the presence of actual angels. You can see their expressions turn skeptical, and I can almost see their minds coming up with rational explanations. But I don't care! Those men—or rather, those angels—gave me such a strong feeling of the presence of God that I will never doubt. I will always remember and give thanks to him."[1]

A Closer Look

For the record, we don't doubt the presence of angels. In fact, we're happy to admit we've absolutely come to believe in angels.

It's not as though we used to think they're imaginary. We accepted their existence, in a theological and theoretical kind of way. But now we truly believe in angelic participation and involvement in the lives of ordinary people. We're convinced that angels surround us every moment of every day.

What won us over? Neither of us has personally seen an angel—though we're certain angels have seen and protected *us*. So what influenced our thinking?

You. Or people like you. And, most assuredly, people like Leroy and Fran Lane.

Not long ago we coauthored a book called *Heaven and the Afterlife,* which examined topics like heaven, hell, angels, demons, ghosts, and other facets of the spiritual realm. Part of the writing process involved many interviews as we collected real-life testimonies. As the amazing accounts poured in, we discovered we had far more than we could share in one book.

A year later we began work on *Encountering Heaven and the Afterlife.* We put out a call for more stories and were overwhelmed with the hundreds that came in. Many were based upon angel sightings—gripping, thrilling firsthand reports.

From these, two common facts emerged: (1) accounts came from credible, rational, clear-thinking individuals; and (2) people who had angelic encounters could never be talked out of their experience. They were entirely convinced. In short, they firmly believed angels had visited them.

We would come to believe them also.

Some of the most astonishing accounts involved not merely seeing but in some cases even interacting with angels. We knew the Old Testament mentions *angel* or *angels* more than a hundred times, and the New Testament nearly twice that number. We were aware that church history is replete with accounts of angelic involvement and that these were demonstrated most notably through the artistry of the Middle Ages. But we were not prepared, quite frankly, for the frequency of the encounters that occur today.

A few examples:

- Coming to the late-night rescue of Martha Cabot and her granddaughter at a Fort Worth theater parking lot, two angelic beings frightened away gang members intent on robbery or worse. When Martha turned to thank the rough and rugged "men" who'd suddenly appeared to provide help, they just as instantly vanished.

- Teenager Carly Kilander, stricken with terminal cancer, had numerous angelic visitors spanning several months. She described some as children and others as adults in appearance. She died on March 16, 2004, comforted and assured of her eternal destination in part because of the "friends" who had come to her during a time of great anguish and pain.

- When four-year-old Kennedy Buettner drowned and died—rather, had a near-death experience—he vividly recalled being snatched up out of the pool by an angel and escorted to heaven. After a mind-boggling tour, he was brought back to his body and resuscitated. He had a full recovery *and* an amazing story to tell.[2]

Again, these are only three out of hundreds. Are angels for real? For starters, they definitely are to those who saw them. Just try to persuade one of those people that angels don't exist. You'll be in a losing battle, and do you know why? Because angels *do* exist, and they've been interacting with humans at various levels for at least thousands of years.

Angels on Assignment

So what exactly do these heavenly beings do? Why do they come to touch earth and its inhabitants? Part of the answer is supplied by stories like the ones in this book: They help accomplish and achieve God's miracles.

Further, the angelic job description is encapsulated in the word that's translated *angel,* which literally means "messenger." Not surprisingly, angels deliver messages: They bring information from God to people. Sometimes the message might be conveyed by their mere presence.

Joshua encountered a strong, imposing figure who was likely an angelic being (although it might have been an appearance by God himself). Joshua asked if he was an ally or an enemy—in effect, saying, "Are you on our side or theirs?" With sword drawn, the angel identified himself as "commander of the army of the Lord" and went on to say he wasn't there to take sides but to take over.[3]

Daniel met a similarly impressive being and, since he was very imposing, fell to the ground at the sight *and sound* of the indescribably intimidating figure before him. Friends with

Daniel at the time were so overwhelmed that they couldn't even look at the angel—they ran for their lives and hid like children. Even he couldn't absorb the sight for long, by his own description turning "deathly pale" and falling facedown.[4]

Whatever these examples have in common, the reasons for the manifestations were notably different. In Joshua's case, the angel apparently appeared to announce that he, the angel, was in charge. With Daniel, the overpowering persona brought a message that included his having been delayed three weeks by demonic resistance.[5]

So in addition to our perception of angels as protectors and rescuers, they also bring news from God to people. Who hasn't sung "Angels We Have Heard on High"? Though the second line begins with "sweetly singing," it's not their musical ability that compels their inclusion in holiday plays and cards. It's what they've said: For instance, an angel informed Mary of Christ's coming birth . . . told shepherds that the birth had taken place . . . instructed Joseph that the baby boy was to be named *Jesus*.[6]

Angels and Humans

The idea that when people die they become angels is an inexplicable myth that has developed and spread, perhaps in part from a misreading of Mark 12:25, which says believers who die "will be like the angels in heaven." Conversely, the rest of the verse provides context: Jesus is speaking of marriage and revealing that we won't be married as on earth. In *that* regard people and angels will be alike.

178

Angels are angels and always will be. People are people and always will be. Though they're far from identical, there are some similarities. Angels and people both

- are creatures made by God
- have distinct and unique personalities
- exist in space and time (angels have considerably more freedom to move in and out of our known space and time)
- have power (angels have superhuman strength yet aren't all-powerful like God)
- possess understanding (angels know more than humans do but aren't omniscient—they long to know things they don't fully understand[7])

There are also significant differences:

- Humans have visible bodies, whereas angels can have visible bodies (or appear to have bodies) or can remain unseen.
- Angels serve humans; humans do not serve angels.[8]
- Humans initially were made lower than angels but eventually became equal with them.[9]

———⌘———

A final point about angels, especially as it relates to miracles: Apparently there are lots and lots of them roaming the earth and watching over us. John, in one of the Bible's most complicated sections, may have seen a hundred million—that's

100,000,000.[10] One thing is clear: An abundance of angels is ready and able to deliver messages and miracles.

If you ever feel alone and abandoned, if you ever feel desperate and despondent, remember that angels aren't far away. That's not a fairytale or movie concept. It's reality. And there's an even more encouraging and energizing reality: The God who created angels also is ready and able—and eager—to help you in times of trouble.

13

MIRACLE MONGERS: PHONIES AND FRAUDS

BEWARE OF SCAMS AND SCHEMES IN GOD'S NAME

In the movie *Leap of Faith,* Steve Martin plays Jonas Nightengale, a fast-talking preacher who travels the country raking in money by deceiving audiences with staged miracles. Unexpectedly, a crippled teenage boy is genuinely healed at one of his rallies. Confronted by the real thing, Jonas starts to question his actions.

The night after the healing rally, Jonas enters the dark, empty tent and stares up at a giant crucifix of Jesus. "Hey, boss. Remember me? Jack Newton," he says, using his real name. "Got a question for you. Why did you make so many suckers?" He then turns to the empty chairs and mimics his own preaching. "You say love never endeth? Well, I say love never stops! You say the meek shall inherit the earth? And I say the only thing the meek can count on is getting the short end of the stick! You say, is there one among you who is pure in heart? And I say, no one!"

Then a voice comes out of the darkness: "Rev."

Nightengale turns to see Boyd, the healed boy, walking toward him. "Hello, Boyd. Why aren't you out signing autographs? Or dancing?"

"I need to ask you a question. Um, I want to know when you plan to leave town." Boyd sits on one of the chairs.

Nightengale steps down from the platform. "Leave? A couple of days, I guess."

"Well, I wanted to know if I could go with you. I could do a lot of things. I'll earn my keep."

He smirks. "You're a little too old to be running away with the circus, aren't you, kid?"

"It's not that. You made me walk again. A lot of people tried to do that, but they couldn't."

"Hold it, kid—I had nothing to do with your walking."

"Sure you did. Everybody saw it."

"Look, I run a show here. It's a lot of smoke and noise and is strictly for suckers. I've been pulling one kind of scam or other since I was your age." He sits down in front of Boyd. "And if there's one thing I know, it's how to spot the genuine article. Because that's what you got to watch out for. Not the cops. You can always get around the cops. But the one thing you can never ever get around is the genuine article. And you, kid, are the genuine article."

"Are you saying you think you're a fake?"

"I know I'm a fake."

"Well, what difference does it make, if you get the job done?"

Nightengale leans forward and says, solemnly, "Kid, it makes all the difference in the world."

Eventually he quits his life as a con-artist.[1]

Throughout the ages, there have been more false claims of healings and other miracles than any person could count. You may recall the fictitious *Elmer Gantry*, a satire whose central character was an unethical, alcoholic minister and evangelist. Ever since its publication, *Elmer Gantry* has been synonymous with ungodly, phony pulpit behavior.[2]

Over the years there have been plenty of real-life Elmer Gantrys and Jonas Nightengales. While we believe we've gone to great lengths to verify the stories presented in this book, not everyone does the same due diligence to confirm authenticity. Let's look at just a couple of those who have succeeded in hoodwinking the public even as they've failed profoundly to glorify God and exemplify his character.

"The Gifted Marjoe Gortner"

In the late 1940s, Marjoe Gortner was a well-known preacher, with a twist: He was only a child. By age four, trained and prodded by his parents, he was proclaimed "the world's youngest ordained preacher." The child evangelist performed on stage, drawing crowds of followers and believers.

However, there's an enormous difference between a trained and committed preacher and a preschooler who's *acting* like a preacher. Unfortunately, the masses swept up in his influence didn't make this distinction. They knew nothing of his parents' motives.

The family traveled all over America, selling "holy" scam objects that supposedly would bring healings and miracles.

At age sixteen, when his father made off with millions of dollars in proceeds, Gortner became disillusioned and abandoned the preaching ministry. But it's not easy to turn away from fraudulent success. A few years later he resuscitated the charade, and phony revivals once again brought him fame and fortune.[3]

Years beyond that, perhaps due to a more awakened conscience—or maybe just looking for another angle to work—Gortner invited a film crew to follow him on tour. Backstage and in hotel rooms, he explained his con-man practices on camera. The result was an award-winning, behind-the-scenes exposé of how easily a charlatan can deceive. His faithful followers didn't realize they were part of the show until the documentary was released.[4]

I (Jim) am a pastor who values and cherishes this calling. Over my forty-plus years of service, I've known, served alongside, or interacted with countless pastors, preachers, and evangelists who've been authentic persons of high character and, like me, viewed our service as a trust given to us.

Thus I find it particularly odious when someone hides behind a veil of ministry to con others. The one thing every spiritual leader should bring to that role is integrity, the most important gift we can contribute. Lack of integrity is unacceptable in any profession but exceedingly problematic and repellent when it occurs among pastors.

Once, after watching a pastor/evangelist—we'll call him Pastor Smith—portrayed on a TV documentary as a scam artist, I called a good friend who knew this man, the alleged scammer. Questioning the accuracy of the reporter, or at least the report, I asked, "Is Pastor Smith for real, or is he bogus?"

There was a long pause. Slowly and softly, my friend answered, "I don't know."

That said it all. My friend had known Pastor Smith for years but could not say if the man's ministry was authentic. Pastor Smith clearly hadn't demonstrated integrity.

My heart was deeply saddened—and angered. Maybe there aren't many Pastor Smiths out there, but they're still around, and they scandalize the vast majority who strive to walk (and not just talk) with integrity.

We must also distinguish between, for example, the serial adulterer and the leader who stumbles into a moral failure but acknowledges wrongdoing, truly repents and recommits to a godly lifestyle. On the one hand are calloused liars bent toward ongoing deception. On the other are sincere believers who have erred, admitted their guilt, repented, made restitution, and become restored. Whether or not these latter return to ministry, the difference between the two categories is profound.

Again, the reality of so-called miracle workers perpetrating deliberate falsehood is nothing new. Phonies and frauds have been around almost as long as the real deal. Jesus said that such people *would* come and deceive many in his name:

Watch out for false prophets. They come to you in sheep's clothing, but inwardly they are ferocious wolves. . . . Not everyone who says to me, "Lord, Lord," will enter the kingdom of heaven, but only the one who does the will of my Father who is in heaven. Many will say to me on that day, "Lord, Lord, did we not prophesy in your name, and in your name drive out demons and perform many miracles?" Then I will tell them plainly, "I never knew you. Away from me, you evildoers!"[5]

While occasionally a false prophet's miracles are genuinely supernatural (based upon God's sovereignty), these acts come from the hand of God's enemy. Most of the time, nothing miraculous takes place at all. The entire event, whatever it is, happens only as pure performance.

"Pop" Goes Peter Popoff

The "faith healer" Peter Popoff serves as a sad example. During his services, Popoff supposedly received supernatural words of knowledge and prophecy about the emotional, physical, and spiritual needs of audience members, including specific ailments and even home addresses. According to published reports, "divine revelations" were actually obtained through a hidden microphone and earpiece. Popoff's wife read information written on prayer request cards or obtained it by talking with people in the audience ahead of time.[6]

Popoff's stage trickery was exposed by the Committee of Skeptical Inquiry in 1986. James Randi tells of Popoff maintaining that his insight was a gift from God. Popoff also accused his critics of participating in a work that made them tools of Satan. Initially he denied using gimmicks but later confessed, "My wife *occasionally* gives me the name of a person who needs special prayers."[7]

Although exposure brought down Popoff's popularity for a time, he made a comeback and continues in late-night TV ministry. Among other things, his return demonstrates tragically that plenty of people are willing to be duped. In an article titled "Peter Popoff, Holy Water, and Financial Seeds Network," one researcher said:

One of Peter Popoff's latest scams is his free "miracle water"—supposedly from Israel (as if that makes any difference to its real holiness or effectiveness)—which can apparently now be "supersized." He gives instructions to drink the holy water, and in five days God will bless the recipient with lots of money. But before this, you need to send Popoff a check as a "seed." He also encloses a bag of "sacred Dead Sea salt" (sacred?!) that you're supposed to sprinkle over a check and send it to Popoff too.[8]

Even today you can order "Miracle Spring Water" *and* a Debt Canceling Kit from Popoff's website.

Whether or not Peter Popoff has sincerely repented and now participates in God-sourced miracles, we don't honestly know, but it certainly seems that the shenanigans continue. Inarguably, his fakery has caused much damage to the reputation of Christianity and through the eyes of many has tainted the splendor of authentic miracles.[9]

Analyzing Miracles: The Catholic Way

We recommend that every supposed miracle be carefully evaluated. In our view, no group invests more to intentionally investigate miracles than the Catholic Church. Consider the process Catholicism follows in the study of the allegedly miraculous.

The Catholic Church has an organization, the Congregation of the Causes of the Saints, headquartered in Rome for the purpose of analyzing miracles. Like most elements of the Roman Catholic tradition, this particular organization has been in existence for centuries, with its precedent institution's origin dating back to 1588.

Congregation in this sense does not refer to a group of people meeting together on Sundays to worship. It's an assembly of investigators charged with analyzing whether alleged miracles are in fact genuine. Specifically, they're tasked with documenting and establishing the evidence for a claim.

The procedure essentially develops as follows:

- A faithful Catholic claims to have asked a deceased saint to pray for healing or a similar miracle, thereby to represent them before God.
- The petitioner was healed or some miracle occurred.
- The petitioner believes God brought the healing as the result of the specific intercession or of the deceased person's prayer.
- A bishop from the region where the deceased leader lived convenes a "court" (group for scientific inquiry) to ascertain whether or not the claim is valid.
- Evidence on both sides of the issue is presented and examined.
- For the healing/miracle to be considered valid, it must be:
  scientifically unexplainable: there can be no natural explanation
  spontaneous and instantaneous: there can be no potential "causes," and it cannot have occurred over a period of time
  perfect: a healing must be complete
  lasting: it cannot be temporary but must continue

- People who argue *against* function as the "devil's advocate." They prepare to dispute the alleged miracle, which, for validation, must undergo and survive the toughest scrutiny. In addition to clerics, the team consists of medical doctors, nurses, eyewitnesses, and others scientifically trained and involved in presenting, hearing, examining, and defending or debunking the supposed miracle.

- The Congregation formalizes their conclusions and sends them to the Pope.

- If the miracle is deemed legitimate, the Pope has discretion as to whether the person who served as intercessory vessel for the miracle can be declared a saint.

Most or all of this seems foreign to non-Catholics. Also, Protestants commonly feel discomfort at this definition of *saint,* believing that the New Testament declares all who truly follow Christ to be saints. Nevertheless, given the world's many Marjoe Gortners and Peter Popoffs, we ought to admire the Catholic Church's diligence in verifying or discrediting miracles and respect its arduous process for determining authenticity.

What about us—what is it that *we* can or should do toward determining whether a healing or other miracle is legitimate? We think highly of the simple—as opposed to simplistic—method that was followed by John Wimber, a true student of healing.[10]

Wimber taught that a person claiming to be healed shouldn't quickly make bold declarations. Conversely, he suggested the following:

- Go to the medical community and request that they run tests.

- Continue taking prescribed medications until a doctor confirms they're unneeded.

- Give the presumed healing ample time. Make no immediate claims that could prove premature. Wait. See if what you're seeing as the miracle truly persists.

If physicians give confirmation through appropriate analysis, if the person can stop taking medications (under supervision) without complications, and if time elapses with the healing still being manifested, *then* he or she can announce, "I am healed."

Let us tell you about someone who did experience a miracle, confirmed by much the same process. Even though we've been highlighting the dangers of frauds and phonies—and there's no shortage—the positive message is that legitimate, genuine healers do exist. They heal in the name of God and give all credit to him. Thankfully, Jimmy Craig, featured below, found someone with a bona fide healing gift.

Modern-Day Miracle: "The Lame Shall Walk . . ."

For the first time in three-and-a-half years, Jimmy Craig left his wheelchair at home and headed to his neurosurgeon's office for an appointment. This wasn't a regularly scheduled checkup; a development in his case needed immediate attention.

Under a clear-blue sky in early January 2004, Jimmy parked his truck and walked inside. While people around him hurried to and from their cars or rushed distractedly through the corridors, Jimmy savored each step, aware of every sensation in his body—the muscles flexing in his legs, the pressure of the ground pushing upward on his feet, the soothing motion of his arms swinging at his sides.

In the examining room, he started to tell his doctor, a renowned neurosurgeon, what had happened to him, what God had done. But the sight itself was far more persuasive than words: Here *stood* a patient who had been irreversibly paralyzed from the waist down, for whom there'd been no known remedy and no hope of recovery.

Overwhelmed and speechless, he gave Jimmy a heartfelt hug. Then, in the face of a confounding medical mystery, he followed his training and ordered an MRI to get a look at Jimmy's spine.

When the results came back, they stood side by side at the lighted wall where the film hung for examination. The doctor was simply dumbfounded.

"He almost fell over backward," Jimmy recalled. "He was seeing two things that couldn't both be true. On the one hand, I was standing right beside him, and on the other the MRI showed there had been no physical change in my condition at all. According to the evidence, I was still crippled. I was a living, breathing impossibility."

The neurosurgeon briefly left the room and returned with two colleagues. With no explanation, and without introducing Jimmy, he asked them to examine the films of the damaged spine and give a diagnosis. Each quickly reached the obvious conclusion: This patient is a paraplegic who will never regain any movement.

"When he told them *I* was the subject of the MRI, and that it had been taken that day, they thought it must be some kind of joke," Jimmy said. "They wouldn't believe it at first. I showed them my driver's license to verify my name as it appeared on the film. Finally, they both admitted there was no scientific explanation for what they were seeing. It had to be a miracle."

On June 19, 2000, Jimmy Craig had been recovering in a hospital room after a relatively routine back surgery called a laminectomy. It was intended to repair a slight injury he had suffered on the job as a carpenter for the San Diego School District. Jimmy had undergone a similar operation once before, with a smooth and full recovery. He had no reason to suspect this time would be any different.

Within hours of the procedure, Jimmy was already taking tentative steps under a physical therapist's direction. The signs were good.

But then he collapsed in blinding pain. Without warning, he lost all feeling and function in his legs.

Staff immediately tried to contact Jimmy's surgeon. Three agonizing days went by before he returned their calls; later investigation would reveal that he had "nicked" Jimmy's spinal cord inadvertently. Instead of assuming responsibility and instantly taking steps to minimize the accident's impact, though, he'd chosen to finish his work, close the incision, and hope for the best.

What Jimmy got was the very worst.

"The pain was on a level I'd never experienced or even heard of," he said. "They were giving me double doses of morphine, but nothing even took the edge off." His agony, which persisted for several weeks, was caused by a blood clot that had formed in the spinal canal. The resulting nerve damage was permanent: Jimmy was done walking.

Before the surgery he'd led an active life. He loved the hard physical work of carpentry. He ran regularly; he was an infielder who'd recently won the church league batting title; he enjoyed snorkeling with his sons and his brother. Now, even after his pain became manageable, Jimmy knew his life would never be the same. Still, he saw no reason to let it be ruined, despite the disability.

"I never once took on a 'woe is me' attitude," Jimmy said. "I never questioned God's plan. Instead of focusing on what I could not do, I focused on what I *could* do. I developed a passion for cooking that's still thriving to this day. And I knew I had to do as much physical activity as I could."

He swam regularly as part of his physical therapy. He learned to drive again in a specially adapted car. In short, Jimmy decided to be the "best paraplegic" he could be and make the most of his opportunities.

———∞∞∞———

Thirty-six months later, Jimmy's son Zach invited him to a gathering at Foothills Church in El Cajon, California, where he attended. The service would feature a guest speaker whose ministry focused on the gifts of the Spirit, including healing. Zach, who'd recently rededicated his life to Christ, clearly was excited at the idea that God might do a miracle for his father.

"I'd been a Christian my whole life," Jimmy said, "but my faith was not at a point where I was ready to believe I could be healed. I knew how messed up I was and that no one had ever come back from my type of injury. Emotionally

I'd accepted my life as a disabled man. I know that sounds strange, but I think it was safer for me to accept the disability than the disappointment of not being healed."

Nevertheless, Jimmy agreed to go, mostly to encourage Zach in his renewed relationship with God. After arriving early to meet up, together they found their way inside and took a front-row seat left of stage. The sanctuary slowly filled, and the room buzzed with conversation. Despite himself, Jimmy began to feel potential in the air and an excitement at the possibility that healing might be what God had in mind after all.

When the Foothills pastors made their way to the stage, accompanied by the guest minister, Jimmy looked at the man and was surprised to see a familiar face.

"His name was Marc Dupont. He'd worked for me years earlier as a contractor," Jimmy said. "I remember sitting on a roof with him in La Jolla, after his father died. He cried and said he didn't think being a roofer was what God intended for him. We prayed together and concluded that his life should be in ministry. We lost touch after that, and now here he was, twenty-three years later, getting ready to lead the healing service."

Before everything began, Dupont, recognizing Jimmy as well, approached for an embrace. On hearing Jimmy's story, he called over a few pastors and other leaders. They anointed Jimmy with oil and—along with some people gathered nearby—they prayed, asking God to touch him and heal his legs. It was fervent, yet as the minutes passed Jimmy realized he wasn't going to just stand up and walk as everyone watched.

"I really expected something to happen, but when it didn't I started to feel bad for my son," he recalled. "He'd acted in faith by asking me to come. I didn't want anything to discourage him in his young walk with the Lord."

Dupont and the others eventually departed to continue with what Jimmy called "the planned service." Within minutes, however, his disappointment was gently pushed aside by a sensation he hadn't experienced in years. He felt a sudden surge of "strength" in his legs. Touching them, as he frequently did to massage away their spasms, he discovered healthy, toned muscles in place of the atrophied ones he'd learned to accept.

"I asked Zach to feel my legs too, because he often massaged them for me and knew how small they'd become. He was amazed and asked what was happening. I said I didn't know. My legs suddenly felt the way they did before the surgery."

Moments later, Jimmy "knew" he could stand up. Zach offered to help, but Jimmy said he was certain he wouldn't need it. No one else appeared to notice when the crippled man for whom they'd earnestly prayed minutes earlier stood up from his wheelchair. Father and son were sobbing with joy as Jimmy stood there, steady and strong, as if he'd just finished an invigorating hike.

Then he walked. Still unnoticed, he walked around the back of the sanctuary—twice—thanking and praising God through his tears with every step for this priceless gift. As he completed the second "lap," Marc Dupont and several others saw him at last.

"Marc walked up to me and said that during the prayer he had seen Jesus lean over and kiss me on the head."

Jimmy doesn't recall the rest of the service, or how the congregation responded, or what anyone else said to him. He was oblivious to everything but his joy—"absolutely basking in the glory of what God had done." Within minutes of his first steps he called his wife, Kelly, and told her the wonderful news.

———∾∾∾———

Jimmy returned home around midnight. His daughter Meghan, twenty-one at the time, had been born with Down syndrome, yet she knew a miracle when she saw one. As Jimmy stepped from his truck, she rushed to meet him and leapt into his arms.

He held her a long time. Then, together, they ran down the street and back, laughing and crying.

"It seemed to me that everything in creation that night was in awe of what God had done," he said. "I embraced my wife—*standing up*—for the first time in three-and-a-half years. It felt like being junior high sweethearts again."

Jimmy still endures persistent numbness and also spasms from a secondary condition caused by his injury. Even so, he's aware every day that he is a "blessed man," and he prays that others will be blessed by his story.

"What God did in my life is an indisputable miracle—to this day doctors look at my test results and have no idea why I'm walking. People ask me how I know it was God who healed me and not just some random or spontaneous event. I tell them I know because, technically, I'm still lame! According to the medical evidence I really haven't been 'healed' at all—yet God made me walk. You can't argue with that."

14

WHAT'S OLD IS NEW

MIRACLES FROM ERAS PAST GIVE US HOPE FOR THE PRESENT

Sitting in Sunday morning service, listening to her pastor talk about miracles, Natalie Jager remembered something she hadn't thought about in years: a dramatic event that oddly had slipped her mind. Intriguing that she'd recall it now, at a time when her faith felt so low and she was so in need of answers.

The first miracle she needed was for a friend battling cancer. She also needed a job, which would require a second miracle.

Here she was, though, thinking of a night two decades ago.

Natalie looked at her husband, Todd, as if to bring the memory also to him, but he was listening intently to the message. She saw the forehead worry lines that were just a little deeper than a year ago, before things got tight financially. Not wanting to disturb him, she pursed her lips and constrained herself, pondering her thoughts.

———∞∞∞———

The year was 1989. Natalie had just finished college and moved to Conroe, Texas, to be near family. She'd spent the evening visiting a friend in downtown Houston, and now it was time to make the forty-five-mile drive back to her townhouse.

She looked at her watch and saw 2:00 a.m.

Fog had rolled in. And not just a hazy mist; it was as dense as any she'd ever seen.

Natalie pulled her Ford onto the freeway and realized she could barely see twenty feet ahead. The trip usually took forty minutes—in good weather, when she could drive seventy-five. She wondered how long it would take while creeping along at twenty, tops. She guessed at least three hours.

The fog seemed to close around her even more thickly. She considered pulling over and parking on the roadside for the night, but the thought of a semi-truck barreling blindly into her car kept her driving. Before long she was hunched toward the windshield, white-knuckling the wheel, squinting into the dark gray . . . and praying hard.

"Dear God, please get me home safe," she prayed over and over again.

She began searching for the faint glow of a neon sign she knew was coming up. The Burger King at the next exit was a landmark she'd passed many times. If she could make it just that far she could pull into its deserted lot and gather her wits. Sleeping in her car seemed safer than the treacherous highway.

Natalie was scared. But even in the midst of fear she knew God could answer her prayer and bring her safely home. After all, hadn't he helped her just two months earlier when she needed a big answer so she could graduate on schedule? Literally just hours from the deadline to pay a $3,600 bill that would keep her from marching with her class, she was sobbing, prayerfully telling God how disappointed she was to miss participating in the ceremony she'd worked so hard to experience. Five minutes later, her phone rang, and she heard her mother's voice: "I'm depositing $3,600 in your account this morning!"

Natalie was flabbergasted. She knew her family didn't have that money to spare. "Where . . . where did you get $3,600?" she stammered.

"Your grandmother's podiatrist gave it to her with the message, 'Tell Natalie congratulations on graduating from college!'"

What were the odds of that happening, and at that precise moment? She considered it a miracle.

Now, still peering into the frightening wall of fog, Natalie strained to see the familiar shape and colors of the neon sign.

She looked at the clock on her dashboard: 2:20. She'd been on the road just twenty minutes. *Where* was that *sign*? Even driving this slowly—she'd kept an eye on the speedometer and knew she hadn't accelerated—it still was hard to believe reaching the next exit would take this long.

She saw a faint glow in the mist. Soon she could almost make out the neon colors.

Thank you! She'd made it.

Steering toward the light, though, Natalie did a double take. This wasn't Burger King. That was the Holiday Inn sign.

The Holiday Inn wasn't even in Houston. It was in Conroe, at the exit nearest her townhouse.

Seeing that sign, she knew what it meant. She wasn't in Houston anymore. She had, in fact, arrived home.

Natalie looked at her dashboard clock again.

The time was 2:25. She had been on the road exactly twenty-five minutes.

When she got home, the first thing she did was call her friend, whose house she had left at exactly two o'clock.

"You're home *already?*" he said. "That's impossible. It's a forty-minute drive at freeway speeds in good weather. How fast did you drive?"

"Twenty miles an hour."

Natalie knew *what* God had done for her, even if she didn't know *how* he did it or even *why*. What he had done was simple: He had somehow picked up her little car in Houston and set it back down in Conroe, just minutes from her house. Some people would call it "instant transport," when the laws of physics are circumvented. In the process, God had spared her from making a three-hour trip in the middle of the night in hazardous driving conditions.

"I know what some people might say, and I'd probably say it too," she commented. "They'd say, 'How do you know you didn't just get disoriented in the fog? Anyone could lose track of the time and distance under those circumstances.' But I know the exact time I left, the distance from point A to point B, and how slowly I was driving. It was a mathematical impossibility—from an earthly perspective."

Natalie looked once again at Todd, and this time he felt her gaze. He smiled and reached for her hand.

That miracle had come when she was young and full of faith—before life had thrown her more than a few challenges. Before she'd watched tragedies unfold and seen suffering go unrelieved and unexplained. In the past twenty years, her faith had taken a beating. She'd been struggling to believe God for what she needed.

But now, recalling the nearly invisible highway—and the graduation money—Natalie felt her faith begin to stir and stretch, like a strong and beautiful creature emerging from a long hibernation.

Everything was going to be okay. She suddenly knew it. God had taken care of her before; he wouldn't stop now. She didn't know how, yet whatever way he chose to respond, she'd been reminded she could trust his loving heart and mighty hand. If he was big enough to move a car dozens of miles, he could handle pretty much anything.

She squeezed her husband's hand. She couldn't wait till they were outside and she could tell him the good news.

A Closer Look

This is, of course, a book about modern-day miracles—emphasis on *modern*. Stories like Natalie Jager's reassure us that extraordinary moments of supernatural intervention still occur. It is worthwhile to pause and realize that people like Natalie—and others profiled in these pages—are part of a long, unbroken string of miracle recipients (and miracle performers) throughout history.

So what about the "not-so-modern" miracles? We know about the miracles of the Bible. What do we know about those from AD 100 (time of the writing of the final book of the New Testament) and today? What can we learn from long-ago miracle workers?

It is likely no surprise that there is a two-thousand-year history of profound and awe-inspiring miracles. Since this is not a history book, we cannot cover many of them. But allow us to take you by the hand and go for a brief walk through history.

God's Power Through Saint Patrick

Originally arriving in Ireland as a slave, Patrick (398–461) eventually would come to have a holiday named after him. He fled from his master in response to a vision and by ship went back to his home and loved ones in Britain. Later, he obeyed dreams from God to return to Ireland with the gospel of Jesus Christ, and a Christian church became rooted in that Celtic land.

During the spring of 433, druids performed magic by the power of evil spirits (unbeknownst to them) and impressed Ireland's King Laoghaire. Patrick challenged them to a contest of "whose-god-is-the-strongest," similar to the biblically described Mount Carmel confrontation between Elijah and the prophets of Baal.[1]

On the Hill of Slane, where Patrick and his followers came together for Easter Vigil, he started a fire for the service, ignorant of the law that no fire could be lit until the beacon on Royal Hill was illuminated. The druids warned the king in prophetic fashion that the fire must be put out right away or it would consume Ireland. The king called for Patrick, asking him to explain himself. Patrick answered by presenting his Christian beliefs.

At that time, Drochu, a head druid, made sport of these claims. Patrick prayed in front of all that Drochu be punished for his blasphemy. Suddenly Drochu was swept up into the air and dropped to the ground, where he died instantly. The king's soldiers tried to arrest Patrick, but he prayed they would be stopped. A dark cloud and a whirlwind came upon them and in the ensuing panic many met their doom.

King Laoghaire backed off, then, even inviting Patrick and his friends to a special banquet. Guests were taken aback when they moved and transported through locked doors before arriving in the banquet hall.

Patrick was offered a drink that Locat-Mael, another head druid, had poisoned. But Patrick sensed what was happening, made a sign of the cross over the cup, and caused the cocktail to freeze while the poison remained in liquid form. He poured out the poison, re-blessed the cup, and drank.

Losing face and wanting to rebuild his reputation, Locat-Mael challenged Patrick to a public display of powers to be held on the plain of Tara.

First he caused thick snow, but Patrick immediately made it go away. Then he brought darkness to the land. When Patrick asked if he could reverse the process, Mael declined. Patrick prayed, and the darkness immediately was extinguished by light.[2]

Are these merely outlandish fables? Could such things actually have happened? Skeptics today dismiss the miracles of Saint Patrick, but the early documents of Ireland described them as unquestionable facts.

Levitation, Instant Transport

Teresa (1515–1582), whose diaries had a sincerity of tone that could convince even a skeptic, made the unusual claim that on occasion she was levitated against her own will.

She indicated this would often happen just as she was ready to take Communion. This was distressing to her as it generated considerable talk among those who observed it.

There are similar accounts from members of the congregation of Alfonso Liguori (1696–1787), who is famous for founding the Redemptionist Order. Liguori levitated while in the middle of a sermon and again while he was praying in his cell. Even late in life, after he became crippled and needed a wheelchair, he lifted off the ground from time to time, once actually hitting his head against the chin of a friar who had been leaning over him.

Liguori's most famous miracle took place in 1774. While getting ready for mass, he fell into a strange trance and didn't snap out of it for two hours. Witnesses experienced something amazing when he awakened, too: He claimed he'd been in Rome, at the bedside of the dying Pope Clement XIV. Parishioners found the story amusing and too far-fetched to take seriously, yet it later was corroborated by others who were with the dying pontiff—they insisted they had not only seen but also conversed with Liguori, who led them in prayer at the deathbed.[3]

How do we interpret such stories? Could they be true? We cannot say. But this we know: The God we serve is great. He is compassionate, he is all-powerful, and he acts according to his will even when we don't grasp or understand it. He will never violate his Word, but he's not obligated to stay within our frame of reference; if he were, he wouldn't be God. He is infinitely above and beyond us, and he reveals what he chooses.

When we read accounts of miracles from hundreds of years ago, we're tempted to dismiss them outright. Beware of doing that. A healthy skepticism is good, even God-given. However, a need to cynically dismiss anything we cannot personally verify is arrogance. God works through many people in the biblical accounts to do remarkable and inexplicable feats. Jesus levitated.[4] Philip was "teleported."[5] Is there a rule somewhere that says Alfonso Liguori or, for that matter, Natalie Jager could not have?

Healing the Infirmed

A frequent feature of Jesus' ministry was compassion for the impaired, including those who could not hear or speak. Others also have healed people with such ailments.

Saint Elizabeth (1207–1231), daughter of King Andrew II and Queen Gertrude of Hungary, did not live very long but had an important, fulfilling life characterized by miracles. Married to Ludwig, count of Thuringia, she experienced a paradoxical world of royalty and humility. She would command her personal servants to wake her for prayer in the middle of the night without bothering her husband. She also came under criticism for being too generous to the needy.

In 1225, a horrible famine hit the land, and Elizabeth used up her own fortune to purchase necessities for the poor, such as grain and other foods. Once she even put a leper in her house—unthinkable at the time—and offered him rest in the very bed she slept in with her husband (even more unthinkable). Ludwig turned absolutely irate but backed off after receiving a vision of Christ crucified.

One day, at a hospital Elizabeth had built, she encountered a deaf and mute boy who was so crippled he could scarcely even move his body to get around town. Not knowing all his specific illnesses, she tried to ask him to describe his predicament, but of course he was unable to answer.

Feeling compassion and assuming he had a demon, finally Elizabeth shouted out, "In the name of our Lord, I command you, and in him that is in you, to reply and to tell me where you came from."[6]

Not only was the boy able to stand up, but, with a voice he'd never used, he also explained how he'd been silent, unable to speak, and deformed since the day he was born.

There are *many* other such accounts as well. We wish we could go into detail about Saint Perpetua of Carthage (181–203), who received a vision that she would endure execution in the Roman arena with calmness and dignity, even in the face of wild beasts. Or Anthony of Egypt (251–356), whose prayers could heal people not in his presence. Or Saint Claire of Assisi (1194–1253), who healed others by making the sign of the cross. Or a host of others whose stories are as amazing as the few we've shared.

The point we're making: God has continued to perform miracles, directly or through others, from biblical times to the present. Another lesson we can take away from this brief excursion through history: The people who received or performed miracles a thousand years ago did so for the same reasons that people experience them today. They lived in eager anticipation that God could and would do extraordinary things through ordinary individuals. They expected miracles to happen—and had faith in the God who delivers them.

That might be what you need to hear right now in your own life. *Expectation* that a miracle really can happen. Along with *faith* that God can deliver it.

15

In the Nick of Time

DOES GOD OFTEN SHOW UP AT THE VERY LAST MOMENT?

Someone once said, "God may not be late, but he misses all the great opportunities to be early."

Doesn't it seem as though God arrives without a second to spare? Or, as for Mary and Martha, does he occasionally get there too late? Martha said to Jesus, "Lord, if you had been here, my brother [Lazarus] would not have died."[1]

Ever had similar thoughts?

If you'd been here, my husband wouldn't have gotten sick....

If you'd been here, our daughter's accident wouldn't have happened....

If you'd been here, we would have been able to keep our home....

Few accounts relate God's apparent penchant for last-possible-moment involvement more jaw-droppingly than the story of Abraham and Isaac. In today's parlance, it was the ultimate close call. This was no father-son getaway or Boy Scout trip. It was three days of walking through a barren wilderness.

On the third day Abraham saw their destination, a mountain in the distance. He told the two servants he had brought to remain with the donkeys and, gathering up the wood he'd split, continued on with Isaac.

He looked at his son. Isaac had been born when Abraham and his wife were well past child-bearing age. The boy had been promised to them. Abraham had trusted God to do the impossible, and his faith had brought him the moniker "Friend of God."

Everyone knew that Isaac's birth was miraculous. But God had told Abraham to take his miracle son atop this mountain and offer him as a sacrifice. And Abraham once again believed God; God would raise Isaac from the dead if necessary. Upward they climbed, Isaac's back now bearing the wood that would become his altar.

At the summit, Abraham laid out the wood and tied his son on top of it. Custom said first to slay the sacrifice by cutting its throat, then to burn the corpse. How could he do such a thing to his son? But how could he *not* obey God's instruction?

With Isaac firmly bound, Abraham raised his knife to finish the deed. With the blade poised in midair, the angel of the Lord suddenly called for him to stop.

"Abraham! Don't harm him in any way. You have shown such fear for God that clearly you would withhold nothing, not even the child he gave you through a miracle."

Then Abraham saw a ram caught in a thicket. He captured it and offered it as a sacrifice in Isaac's place.

Isaac went on to have a son, Jacob, whose name was changed to Israel and who became the father of all Jewish people. For Abraham and Isaac, God came through just in the nick of time. For God, though, there was no "nick"—it was precisely the perfect moment.[2]

No Margin for Error

We've all heard stories like this: "I needed the money by three o'clock or the bank was going to start foreclosure. I got a check for the exact amount at 2:55—*in the nick of time!*"

There's that expression again. God seemingly comes through just in time to prevent catastrophe or crisis. As the deadline races toward us, it figures that our miracle will materialize an instant before the clock strikes.

In the medieval age there was another common term: *pudding time.* Often the first course served, pudding was a savory dish made of sausage and blood. A guest arriving at "pudding time" got there to enjoy the start of the meal. As we know, pudding gradually came to be more of a dessert-type dish eaten toward the end.

A "nick," though, was either a notch cut into a stick—used to tally currency amounts, for example—or a marking on a clock or a musical instrument for accurately telling time and for precise tuning. To say one was "in the nick" would mean one was in exactly the right place at exactly the right moment.

More pressingly: *Does* God wait purposefully until the last minute to come to our aid? *Is* he like a screen hero who rides in to achieve our dramatic rescue? Once again, it sure feels like it to us. But that's because we're looking at things from our perspective.

Those "if you'd been here" thoughts we mentioned above—those are our feelings, our perceptions. Reality is quite another matter.

God is never late. He's truly a *present* (not absent) help in times of trouble.[3]

The Right Thing at the Right "Moment"

Presently we exist in time, one of the dimensions of our known reality, and we'll remain in time, limited by time, for a period of time. Some of us will live seventy-five years, others ninety, and perhaps a few—like Tolkien's Bilbo Baggins—will celebrate an "eleventy-first birthday." In this life, on this earth, everything we'll see and hear and experience will be measurable in the units by which we measure what we know as *time*.

But the eternal God, an uncreated being, is in no way bound by time, whether it's denoted in decades or nanoseconds. Therefore, the truth is it's illogical to say that God "waits until the last minute" for anything. To him, all "minutes" are *now*. There's no past, present, or future outside of time.

God does not "wait" until we're in dire straits to test us or to prove anything to us. God acts at exactly the right moment—*always*. We can trust him to be there when it's the right "time" for him to be there.

We think he moves "at the last minute" because, once we've received the miracle, we're done waiting for it. It's like the saying, "I found what I lost in the last place I looked." Of course you did! After you found it, you stopped looking.

The more poignant question is, then, does God have a purpose in what are, from our perspective, "delayed" miracles?

Throughout history we see example after example of God seeming to move slowly. Often it's out of compassion for people who are in rebellion: God mercifully gives them one opportunity after another to turn to him. And sometimes the apparent delay is for the accomplishment of a greater purpose.

Joseph was one of Israel's twelve sons. His brothers grew jealous of their father's disproportionate affection for him, so they sold him as a slave. In time, Joseph, now in a different land, was falsely accused and thrown into prison, where he sat for years.

Was God *late* in rescuing Joseph? No. Over his long incarceration, a servant of the king came to know that Joseph could interpret dreams, and after the king had a series of nightmares, he was summoned. When he interpreted them, Joseph was elevated to a powerful position and enacted plans that saved not only the king's people but also his family. While it may have appeared that God was tardy in coming to Joseph's side, it was the perfect "timing" for the enactment and, ultimately, the fulfillment of God's purpose.[4]

This illustrates another divine purpose: Sometimes "our" miracle is really a divine intervention for others also. God knows just how—and when—to put it all together so that many can be blessed.

When God Doesn't Show Up "On Time"

We've been sharing stories of God miraculously saving the day for people in a horrific accident, or facing dangerous circumstances, or suffering injury and illness. What about when he doesn't provide a miracle? What about those who have prayed and been prayed for to be healed but aren't? Did God come up short? Was he too late to help?

No.

Again, God isn't limited or insufficient—but our understanding may be. The idea that God has done the wrong thing, or hasn't done the right thing, or has missed the moment, comes from our notion that this life here and now is where it's at—or even all there is.

Yes, many of us say we're convinced of everlasting life. Yes, we confess belief in heaven. And yes, we strive to strengthen our faith in God and his promises. But when it's our turn to feel frantic or forlorn, we sometimes live as though eternity were a myth.

We pray for healing. We trust the miracle will come. If it doesn't, and if this short stay on planet earth is our heart's real treasure, we may wonder whether there's any true basis for our faith at all. Perhaps we'll decide that there isn't and turn away from God.

That, however, is the belief and the act for which there's truly no basis. We do not—*cannot*—place limitations on God.

Furthermore, life doesn't end with "death." The astonishing truth is that God made us eternal beings: We will exist *forever.* When we're done here, there's no "lights out, fade to black." Though physical death will temporarily separate our spirit from our body, it isn't an end but a transition, a passage.[5]

God, always and entirely in the *now* (remember, eternity has no past, present, or future), fully knows what we sometimes refuse to believe and often forget: Death isn't a failure, and it has no finality. To say "God didn't come through in time" is to say we simply haven't yet grasped eternity's true meaning.

It *is* painful to lose a loved one. Pain *is* a part of this life, and not just for those who feel their only hope is an immediate miracle. But pain exists because of our choices, not the Creator's. God didn't design suffering, and he didn't cause it. And the reason pain and suffering are forever going away—will one day be no more—is that God has initiated and will accomplish their ultimate banishment and our everlasting redemption.[6] As only he possibly could. In what will prove to be precisely the right "timing."

There is never any truth to the thought that God is tardy in his plans.

The great king Solomon said, "Trust in the Lord with all your heart and lean not on your own understanding."[7] Our role is to trust. We can then leave the timing to God.

Does God have a flair for the dramatic? Does he arrive at the last possible moment to add thrills and chills to the story? That would presume he needs to be noticed or wants to show off. The reality is that God comes to us not as a performer but as a lover. He wants our hearts to be intimately connected with him. He orchestrates the details of our lives to encourage us consistently toward trust in and love for him.

Waiting for God to act also stretches our faith. In one sense, the longer we wait, the more we're stretched. During those times, as always, he's at work in our lives, often in ways that aren't yet visible.

That was the case with Ray Wallace and his family, who walked forward in faith even though the road ahead was far from clear. The Wallaces saw—and hopefully you will see also—that while God rarely is *early,* he definitely is *on time.*

215

Modern-Day Miracle: The Doors Kept Opening

In the summer of 1985, things were looking *good* for Ray Wallace. He had recently been promoted to U.S. Army Staff Sergeant, he'd just graduated at the top of his intermediate German class at the Defense Language Institute in Monterey, California, and he had orders to join a prestigious intelligence unit in Berlin, Germany. Best of all, he and his wife, Caroline, recently had been blessed with their first child—a beautiful five-month-old boy named Richard.

One problem lurked amid all that good news: Government housing for military personnel with families in Berlin was in short supply. The eleven-month waiting list left Ray little choice but to get in line with everyone else. He'd been told by friends already there that the chances of finding affordable off-post housing were even less promising. His family was welcome to stay with his parents in Texas for as long as necessary, but the prospect of missing nearly a whole year of Richard's young life and of leaving Caroline alone to care for him was unacceptable. This cast a dark shadow over an otherwise exciting and promising opportunity.

The night before his plane left for Germany, Ray dreamed of being in a canoe headed for the edge of a dizzying waterfall. All night long he paddled frantically but still drifted steadily toward the terrifying plunge ahead. He woke before dawn and prayed through sunrise.

"I told God I couldn't believe he'd given me a wonderful wife and beautiful son, just to let us be separated for so long," Ray said. "I asked for a miracle to keep that from happening."

When Caroline awoke, hours before Ray was to leave, they prayed together. She was prepared to summon the courage and

216

patience to weather a lengthy separation. But that morning she left no room for doubt that she wanted God to intervene and make this unnecessary. Like Ray, she asked him to keep her family together, period.

Then Ray experienced a surge of confidence. Kneeling with his wife beside their bed, he made a bold—and illogical—declaration of faith.

"I told Caroline to give me one week to scout things out, and then I'd send for her. I was speaking, but also listening to the words coming out of my mouth, like they were a message meant for both of us. I didn't have any idea how God would do this, but I suddenly just *knew* he would."

A series of serendipitous miracles—not just one, but three—were set in motion that morning and would unfold slowly over the next few faith-testing weeks.

By the time Ray landed in Berlin his confidence had begun to wane. He made it his mission, from day one, to tell everyone he met he was looking for housing. Did anyone know of a lead to follow?

The consistently discouraging answer: *No. Impossible. Forget about it.* Ray learned he qualified for seventeen days lodging in temporary housing, tops. He struggled to quell a rising tide of panic and despair. Still, despite his doubts, he clung to his promise to send for Caroline and Richard within a week.

Seven days later, on a bright, sunny Saturday, nothing had changed. Ray set out to find a German post office where he could call without being overheard in the barracks. He had no idea what he would say—until he heard Caroline's voice across the Atlantic.

"Come," he said. "Book your flight and just come. We'll use the seventeen days of temporary housing and trust God for what comes after that."

Ray hung up, practically shaking. That dream of helplessly canoeing over the waterfall seemed eerily real. To take his mind off of things, he decided to go for a walk along the Kurfurstendamm, Berlin's most famous promenade and shopping district.

Cue *Miracle Number One.*

He hadn't gone far when he came upon a crowd gathered around a street theatre performance. He stopped to watch and quickly recognized the subject of the play: The actors were portraying in mimed movements the crucifixion and resurrection of Jesus. Ray knew enough about German culture to understand the rarity of such a public evangelical outreach. Germans mostly kept religion private, if they affirmed faith at all.

"My face must have been beaming as I watched their beautiful performance," Ray said, "because immediately after, one of the players walked straight up to me and said, 'You're a believer, aren't you?'"

Ray felt like he'd been reunited with long-lost family. His new brothers and sisters invited him to their nearby church later that evening, and he eagerly accepted.

During refreshments after the service, Ray encountered *Miracle Number Two.*

It arrived in the form of a seventy-six-year-old woman named Ruth Krause. She was delighted to meet this clean-cut young American who spoke German so well—and who was a Christian to boot! Their conversation was instantly warm and comfortable. Ray eventually got around to telling her of his search for a place to live, sharing the details about his leap of faith that afternoon.

"Germans usually are very guarded and private, slow to open up to strangers," Ray said. "She didn't know me from Adam, so I nearly fell over when she told me we could live in her apartment for six weeks while she visited her sister in Vienna."

There was one catch: Her vacation didn't begin for another three weeks. But Ray looked at a calendar and realized she was scheduled to leave on the very day his temporary housing expired—the seventeenth day after Caroline was set to arrive.

Ray thanked God and joyfully accepted the offer.

"When my company First Sergeant heard what I'd planned he said to me, 'Son, if you were any younger or any lower in rank I'd order you to call your wife back right now and cancel her flight,'" Ray recalled. "'German people don't just open up their homes like that. There must be some scam involved.' He said he 'hoped to God' I knew what I was doing. I told him I believed the whole thing was God's doing. He had no response to that. To tell the truth, though, I wasn't nearly as sure as I sounded."

———

After Caroline arrived with Richard, she joined Ray in the search for permanent housing. Together they followed every lead. They joined the throngs who swarmed apartment showings. However, being foreigners made them less than desirable to landlords seeking long-term tenants.

"We'd been growing steadily more anxious, but every time we prayed we felt God was telling us to be calm and wait,"

Ray said. "When we got down to only a week left before Ruth's vacation ended, it was all we could do to keep from losing our minds with fear."

With five days left, *Miracle Number Three* landed.

Arriving at the office that morning, Ray saw a message on his desk from the unit operator: *Call Ben Bartlett.*

Puzzled, Ray picked up the receiver and dialed. He and Bartlett had known each other briefly at language school; Ben studied Russian and had been assigned to Berlin a few weeks ahead of Ray. They'd seen each other when Ray arrived, at a unit picnic and softball game, then hadn't crossed paths since.

Ben answered and, after greetings, casually asked, "Still looking for housing?"

You have no idea! Ray thought. He wondered how Ben could know this. Then he remembered: The day he'd arrived he'd told *everyone*—even Ben, as they'd waited in line together for a grilled hamburger. "Yes, I am," he said, practically holding his breath.

"A friend of mine got orders to leave three months earlier than expected. He needs someone to take over his lease. The place is pretty much yours if you want it."

"When?" Ray knew the vacancy probably was weeks away and already his mind was racing to think of some way to cover the interim.

"They're leaving the country next Monday."

Monday. Of course. The day Ruth Krause returned from Vienna. The day Ray and his family would have been facing homelessness and humiliation. The day, instead, that a loving God would finish answering their prayers with a string of improbable miracles.

The deal went through without a hitch. The apartment, spacious and comfortable, was just a ten-minute bike ride from Ray's office. The First Sergeant shook his head and said he'd never met anyone with better luck.

But Caroline and Ray knew that luck had nothing to do with it.

16

ARE SOME PEOPLE "MIRACLE MAGNETS"?

CERTAIN FOLKS SEEM TO ATTRACT SUPERNATURAL ENCOUNTERS

You know you're dealing with people who have experienced many miracles when, at the end of a ninety-minute interview, they say, "Oh, we forgot to tell you about the time our daughter was raised from the dead!"

That's what happened when we spoke with Dennis and Ginger Lindsay from the Dallas offices where they lead Christ for the Nations. They told one story after another of personal involvement with the miraculous. And they could have told dozens more.

"We have seen hundreds—too many to count or remember," Dennis said.

Perhaps this shouldn't surprise us. Dennis grew up in a home with parents, Gordon and Freda, who accepted miracles as part and parcel of their faith. They founded The Voice of Healing Ministry in 1947. Decades later, in the 1970s, Gordon started Christ for the Nations Institute, a Bible teaching and missionary training school. Devout and endlessly active servants of God, the Lindsays were frequent eyewitnesses to miracles—and hardly surprised by them.

"That's the kind of faith my parents had," Dennis remembered. "They just expected God to show up in powerful and extraordinary ways, and he quite often met their expectations."

Dennis began traveling with his dad at age ten. Gordon led healing services and crusades all over the country, and Dennis glimpsed numerous miraculous events.

One involved a boy named Ronnie Coyne, whom Dennis met when Ronnie was twelve. At seven, Ronnie had found some barbed wire and begun playing with it, swinging it around like a lasso. The wire got caught in his right eye like a fish hook.

Within two weeks the eye became infected and had to be surgically removed. Doctors fitted Ronnie with a plastic eye.

In June 1951, Ronnie's family attended a revival and healing crusade at a school in Sapulpa, Oklahoma. Ronnie's mom urged him to receive prayer from the evangelist, Daisy Gillock—not for his eye but for tonsils that were bothering him.

Afterward, when he was walking away, Gillock called out to him, "Wait a minute, son, your eyes are not working properly." She didn't know he had a plastic eye—she just thought he was cross-eyed. She asked, "Do you believe the Lord can heal your eyes?" He said he did. She prayed for him, and he began to see through both eyes. That's right: Ronnie Coyne had vision through his prosthetic eye.

Gordon became acquainted with Ronnie, who began to travel with him to various cities for evangelistic healing rallies held in tents. He would tell the assembled audiences about the boy's miracle and show the crowd how he could see, to bolster their faith. During these testimonies, Dennis would hold Ronnie's eye in his hand.

"They would securely tape up his good eye and ask people to bring something for him to read—a handwritten note, driver's license, or program," Dennis recalled. "Sure enough, he could read everything perfectly—through his plastic eye or his empty eye socket."

Often local newspapers and skeptics of all kinds would test Ronnie in various ways, certain it was a stunt. Not so. Every time, under many circumstances, Ronnie proved he could see out of his right eye.

"I didn't need any convincing," Dennis said. "I was his friend during that time, and I'd seen him demonstrate his miracle eye dozens, maybe hundreds of times."

Eventually, Ronnie left the crusades to continue his schooling. He and Dennis lost track of each other. About twenty years later, Dennis was watching the television show *That's Incredible!* when he heard the announcer say, "Stay tuned. After the break we'll bring you an amazing miracle man who can see without an eye!"

He hurried to record the segment. And then, there was Ronnie, testifying on TV to how the Lord had restored his vision. An optometrist used his equipment to verify that Ronnie was blind in one eye, and he said, "This man's optic nerve has been completely severed, and he can't even tell the difference between light and dark."

The hosts then repeated the display Ronnie had conducted so many times as a boy, asking audience members to give Ronnie something to read, which he did perfectly. They assured viewers no audience members had known of Ronnie before, that no trickery was involved.

—⚬⚭⚬—

In 1974, Dennis and Ginger had returned from missionary service to Spain and were teaching at the Dallas school. They felt God calling them to lead a group of students to minister in Mexico City that summer. Dennis called Wayne Myers, a missionary friend there, to help arrange housing. Wayne asked when they would arrive—sometime in early July—and told them to come to his home. He'd direct them from there.

Months later, they rolled into the area with fifteen students. Dennis unfolded a map and asked Ginger for the last letter from Wayne to get his address. Mexico City already was an enormous metropolis with about fifteen million people.

Dennis looked at the letter and discovered there was no street address, just a P.O. Box number. *Uh-oh. Now what?* Long before the days of cell phones, and lacking a phone number anyway, they all wondered how in the world they would find one little apartment in that massive, sprawling, crowded city. One student, Greg, had worked alongside Wayne the previous year but couldn't begin to point them to their destination. In fact, he couldn't even say which direction they should head.

Dennis decided to pull off the highway, drive onto a city street, and enter the nearest church to ask if, by chance, anyone knew Wayne Myers. Driving a little too fast, he missed his intended off-ramp, which was nothing more than a sharp right turn. Then he missed the next one. Finally, he exited a half-mile farther along than he had planned.

226

On a side street, he stopped and parked to check the map and get his bearings. Looking in the rearview mirror, Dennis spotted a traffic circle (called glorieta) with a fountain in the middle. Mexico City is dotted with these.

"Hey, Greg," Dennis called. "Didn't you say Wayne's home was close to a glorieta? Get out and see if that's the one."

Greg shot a look that said, *Are you crazy? There's no way!* But he said, "Do you know how many glorietas there are here? Must be ten *thousand* throughout the city—they're all over the place." He shrugged and got out to take a look.

Soon everyone heard him whooping and shouting, "This is it! This is it!"

Greg had ridden his bike past this fountain many times, and even though there was nothing unusual about it, he now recognized it.

It turned out the group was *one block* from Wayne's home, which was on a very short street—nearly impossible to find on the huge city map.

A minute later, when they arrived, they found their friend walking through his front gate with travel bag in hand.

"Wow, that's good timing, Dennis!" Wayne said. "I'm just leaving for two weeks up in the mountains. There's no way you could've reached me. You got here in the nick of time."

Finding Wayne's home was like finding a needle in many, many haystacks. That, according to Ginger, was just the first of dozens of miracles the team experienced throughout the summer.

"We wrote them all down in a journal," she said, "and even now we marvel at the amazing things God did almost every day. We should've known it would be that way, since we seemed to arrive at Wayne's home out of nowhere."

In 1995, Dennis and Ginger joined a church history tour through Europe; one of the stops was Paris and its landmarks. They separated from their group to stroll along the Avenue des Champs-Elysées, famed boulevard of outdoor cafés and chic shops. As they enjoyed sights and sounds, they were approached by two ragged-looking girls, around age ten. Their hair was unkempt, their dresses were wrinkled, and they were begging from tourists.

One held a folded-up newspaper. "Please give me money," she would say, waving it in front of her.

Gently, Dennis said, "No, thank you. No." He'd been hounded hundreds of times in dozens of cities and had chosen long ago to give his money to reputable charities.

The girls persisted, following the couple down the sidewalk. Dennis finally became more adamant: "No, no money today." At last, the girls turned and walked away.

It suddenly dawned on him that the group had been warned repeatedly to be on guard against thievery. He looked at Ginger with concern. "Do you think those girls could've been pickpockets?" He checked his pockets and fanny pack, but his passport and everything else seemed to be there. So they shrugged off the encounter and continued walking.

Twenty minutes later, Dennis felt a tap on his shoulder. He turned to see the two girls, one of them waving his wallet.

"You dropped this," she said, handing it to him. Dennis and Ginger stood in momentarily stunned silence.

Sure enough, the girl had been a pickpocket. She'd skillfully used one hand to unzip the pack and remove the wallet while using the newspaper as a screen and distraction. She'd even re-zipped the pack to avoid detection.

The wallet contained everything Dennis had placed there—credit cards, driver's license, and a small amount of cash.

They watched as the girls wandered off. When they asked several merchants if the gypsy kids ever returned wallets, they were met with snickers. "Are you kidding? Never."

"She risked getting caught and reported by chasing me down to return it," Dennis recalled. "She could've just thrown it in the trash. She didn't ask for a reward or anything—just walked away."

Some might call that incredibly good luck. Dennis and Ginger call it a miracle.

———⊱❧⊰———

And about that daughter raised from the dead . . .

In the fall of 1992, Missy began her last year of high school, ready to complete her pre-college studies and excited about playing point guard on the basketball team.

On Sunday, October 4, Dennis and Ginger had a grueling trip that would eventually land them in Cordoba, Argentina, where they were helping to establish a Bible school. Despite their fatigue, they went that evening to a church where Dennis was scheduled to speak. His topic: "God Takes Care of His Children."

They finally collapsed into bed around two o'clock. Almost immediately, the phone rang. On the other end was Christ for the Nations' head of security.

"Your daughter has been hit by a car," he said. "You need to come home right now. She's not expected to live."

Stunned, they got on their knees and prayed for a long time. Then they read Psalm 91, which begins, "Whoever dwells in the shelter of the Most High will rest in the shadow of the Almighty. I will say of the Lord, 'He is my refuge and my fortress, my God in whom I trust.'"

Eventually, Dennis went to sleep, overcome by exhaustion. Ginger stayed awake to continue praying and reading Scripture.

Later they would learn that Missy had been preparing to cross a six-lane road, close to the campus, to meet friends at a café. It was evening and getting dark. When the light where they waited turned green, she was the first among her group to begin walking.

A white Cadillac had raced through the cross-street's red light. Witnesses estimated its speed at between fifty and sixty. The car plowed into Missy.

The force of the front bumper's impact slammed her into the windshield face-first. She then tumbled over the top like a rag doll. Finally, she fell off the back end as the driver sped away, running the next red light as well. No one managed to get the license plate number.

Missy ended up thirty-five feet from the crosswalk, landing on her head. Blood gushed from a gaping wound.

The head of security, whose guard station was nearby, rushed to the scene. Trained in emergency medical techniques, he checked her vital signs—pulse, heartbeat, and breathing. Nothing.

Students gathered around to pray, pleading for God's help. Anxious seconds passed without any success in finding vital signs.

A full six minutes later, Missy took a breath.

Soon, an ambulance arrived to whisk her to the hospital. EMTs cut away clothing so they could start IVs and other procedures. For her part, Missy was still unconscious and in shock.

She was immediately admitted to the ICU for a battery of tests. All came out negative. No broken bones. No damaged organs. No brain injury. Not one thing wrong except extensive bruising and lacerations, and a nasty head gash requiring many stitches.

The physicians were baffled. They told Missy's friends, "We have seen these kinds of accidents and know there must be significant injury."

When Dennis woke on Monday, he quickly called and learned that Missy was unconscious but alive. Though Ginger was ready to get home as soon as possible, they both felt an undeniable urging from God to stay and finish what they had come to do.

"I had tremendous peace that wasn't from me," Ginger said. "I knew I was supposed to stay."

Experiencing complete assurance that Missy was in God's hands, they made the decision to keep in close contact from a distance and remain in Argentina.

Tuesday, doctors decided to redo all the tests, still unconvinced Missy could've come through such a horrific accident relatively unharmed. Again, they found nothing wrong. On Wednesday—not even three days after the accident—Missy was released, told to go home and rest. She walked out on crutches, still sore and wobbly.

Dennis and Ginger are positive God used that terrifying incident to reach Missy. She was essentially alone during the hospital stay and the days following—all family members normally in the area were away. In many hours alone, it was Missy and God.

It's as if she heard him say, "I love you for who you are. I've not let you die because you have a purpose to fulfill, and you haven't fulfilled it yet." She had grown up in a highly visible family of respected evangelists, Bible teachers, and ministry workers—and she was pretty sure she didn't want to follow that path. But her perspective began to change; she felt a calling on her life. Thereafter she went on mission trips every summer and ministered to others. To this day, serving God is her highest goal.

On Saturday, she met Dennis and Ginger at the airport on crutches. As they hugged tightly, they knew God had performed a miracle—in Missy's body and in her heart.

A Closer Look

Do some people "attract" miracles more so than others? If so, why?

In the Paris story above, I (Jim) was there, and I also have known Dennis and Ginger Lindsay for many years. They have personally experienced a *boatload* of miracles. How is that? Why do certain individuals seem to have "miracle magnetism"?

One theory pertains to a specific biblical term: *apostle.* For starters, this word can refer to those who were closest to Jesus: his disciples. Additionally, it refers to those who have established new beachheads for the church, as Paul did while moving the gospel's epicenter westward through his journeys across Asia Minor toward Rome.

There might be another meaning, too—that is, an apostle is one who experiences miracles. If this is correct, then maybe some of those who frequently encounter miracles are present-day apostles. Admittedly, there's heated debate among some theologians and scholars about whether the role of apostle exists today or ended in New Testament times.

If this role *is* still active and if one of the definitions is a person who experiences miracles, then that could explain why miracles occur often in certain people's lives. That would undoubtedly be conveyed by Acts 2:43, which reads, "Everyone was filled with awe at the many wonders and miraculous signs performed by the apostles."

It's worth noting that the apostles did not follow signs and wonders (miracles). Rather, *miracles followed them*. Simply put, God—for reasons unknown to us—showers some persons with the miraculous.[1]

What About the Rest of Us?

You might be saying, "What about me, though? I'm not an apostle and never will be, but I do need a miracle! Can't I have one?" Allow us to say a cautious and reverent *yes*. We affirm that

- God absolutely *can* do the miraculous.
- the childlike (not childish) expectancy that God *will* appear in a miraculous way seems to impact its likelihood. We say this in the sense that faith releases the Spirit of God to do what he does best.

Warning: *This is not a formula*. It isn't some lever to be pulled or button to be pushed. But it is a scriptural principle. Our observation and conviction is that people who expect God to do the inexplicable see more of his inexplicable acts.[2] (If you feel any discouragement right now, or if you're disillusioned, please read on, and see the epilogue for more about God's unceasing, never-ending love for us. For *you*.)

I (Jim) once was speaking at a televised event. Many people spoke, each allotted five minutes rather than the normal thirty to forty. Speaker after speaker went to the podium. Immediately following me was Ken Copeland, who stood and merely said, in the most emphatic, confident, and assertive tone, "Have faith in God."[3] Then he waited. Again he said, "Have faith in God!" with even greater emphasis. After another pause, he said again, "Have faith in God." Pausing once more, he continued, "Have faith in God."

I do not recall how many more times he said this, but as he said it, the reality of his words began to soak into our spirits. I mean *really* soak in. My mind felt like I was experiencing a sanctified version of Churchill's famous "Never, never, never, never give up" speech.

Copeland made his point and sat down. And I've never quite recovered from that moment. When I'm riddled with doubt, I think of his "Have faith in God" speech.[4]

This brings us back to the question: Who experiences miracles? Answer: anyone God chooses to bless with a miracle.

Who seemingly experiences the *most* miracles? Those who expect them the *most*.

Expectancy is an incubator for miracles. Dennis Lindsay, for example, doesn't chase them. He doesn't strain for them. On the contrary, he's quite calm and relaxed in his faith, by nature low-key and understated. But miracles come to him!

What can *we* do? What *must* we do? We're not only to expect God to do what no one else can, but we're also to place no limitations on God. We're to know that God *is*.

Think about that for a moment. God *is*. If that statement is true, what's beyond the realm of possibility for him? God *is*. There's no *is not* to balance that out. God *is* able to do all that needs to be done.

Let us ask you:

- Are you in need of a healing miracle? Remember, God *is*.

- Do you need a financial miracle? God *is*.

- Are you in need of a relationship miracle? God *is*.

- Do you need a job miracle? God *is*.

The Bible tells us God *is* able to do more than we can even dream. That's how big God *is*. Those who see miracles in their lives are people who don't tell God what he can and cannot do. They know—or they will come to know. God *is*.

Ask, and It Shall Be Given

Those we're calling "miracle magnets" are people who don't hesitate to ask God for the impossible. Many others ask only for what is accomplishable by human hands. Perhaps they think it's presumptuous to ask God for what's outside our possibility. But in truth, God wants us to trust him for what only he can do.

Arthur Pierson, pastor of London's Metropolitan Baptist Church, said, "We ask but little, when we should only honor God by making large demands."[5] The "by making large demands" part throws most of us a bit. So let's substitute "by having big expectations."[6]

Learn to have large expectations of God! Let this excite you and make you want to ask him for something really big, something only he can do!

Unbelief tends to release the power of the evil one, whereas faith in God releases the power of his Spirit.[7] Nothing you'll read in this book is more significant than this.

No doubt you've heard the cliché "Seeing is believing." When it comes to miracles, we need to turn that around: Believing is seeing. When you believe God is powerful enough and loving enough to intervene in your life . . . when you believe there's no request too small or too big . . . when you believe miracles are for real . . . then there is no limit, no ceiling, no restriction on what God could accomplish in your life.

Beware of Being a Miracle Chaser

Developing Character Trumps Flashy Spiritual Encounters

Zacharias Morge, an elderly farmer and pastor, lives in the village of Chano Mille, Ethiopia. A simple, humble man, he's in his eighties—though he can't say his exact age because he doesn't know his exact birthday. He's recognized throughout his country as a "Man of God" who spends countless hours on the "prayer mountain" near his home.

Many stories have been told about his close relationship with God, but one of the most miraculous comes from when Ethiopia was controlled by a Communist regime. . . .

One morning, some years ago, Zacharias emerged from his plain mud hut with a mission in mind. Carrying a heavy box, he sidestepped chickens pecking at the dirt road and a few goats wandering about. Passion to share his faith in Jesus with others compelled him to take Bibles to a government administration compound.

Making his way past huts, carts, and little vegetable gardens, he arrived and was met at the gate by a soldier on duty. The guard searched the box and barked, "What are you doing with *these?*"

Zacharias softly replied that he would give them to the office workers there. Incensed, the guard wanted the Bibles destroyed immediately.

A baker's oven stood near the gate. The guard ordered Zacharias to throw all the cherished Scriptures into the blaze.

Zacharias gently but emphatically answered, "This is the Word of God—I will never burn it."

"Either throw the Bibles into the fire," the guard shouted, "or stick your arm into the flames!"

Zacharias could see he meant what he said. He whispered a quick prayer, and then he hesitantly put his arm into the scorching fire.

No doubt the guard expected a shriek of pain and a quick retreat. But Zacharias uttered not a sound. When he slowly removed his arm, there was no sign of injury.

Wild-eyed, the guard yelled, "Again! Put your arm in again!"

Now Zacharias left his arm in the kiln long enough to ignite a piece of wood. Pulling it out once again, he clearly was not burned at all.

Even more bewildered and furious, the guard raged, "Put your arm back in the fire and *leave* it there till I tell you to pull it out."

The elderly man complied. White heat danced around his skin. And again, no sound came from his mouth.

At last the guard told him to remove his arm. Once more, his arm was unscathed.

Just then, the commanding officer walked by and saw the box.

"What are those Bibles doing here?" he roared. *"Throw them into the fire!"*

But the guard raised his hands and said, "Not me. Not after what I just saw."

Infuriated, the officer reached into the box, threw a Bible into the fire, and stormed away through the gate. At this desecration, Zacharias fell to the ground in a faint.

The next day, the officer who had destroyed the Bible died of a head wound caused by a stray bullet while he was walking in a safe zone.

Out of deep humility, Zacharias rarely spoke of the incident. But his missionary friends certainly thought of Shadrach, Meshach, and Abednego, who were thrown into blazing fire for their faith in God yet also emerged without a single singed hair.[1]

A Closer Look

We understand from those who connected us to Zacharias Morge—people who know him well—that he's a man of integrity and truth before he is a man of miracles. That is to say, he's more concerned about the consistency of his faith and the quality of his character than he is with spectacular supernatural moments.

Beware of developing an obsession with miracles. We say this because there are people of faith who chase after sensational, dramatic, emotive spiritual experiences. The problem is their desire for the extraordinary can turn into a pursuit with an increasingly unreasonable and unreachable goal. What's truly most important is ongoing integrity, compassion, and love. From a stock-market-like vantage, a steady trajectory of growth is worth far more than brief spikes.

For this wisdom we can look to the world's best-known book of miracles: John's gospel. It states that Jesus performed many miracles, witnessed by the disciples, that weren't recorded.[2] The Bible isn't intended as a catalogue of miracles.

Jesus himself made clear that "signs and wonders" aren't the key to faith, though some people, without them, would struggle to believe.[3] He praised those who would have faith without seeing him or his miracles in person.[4] The message seems plain: "Believe in me, whether or not you see something that might 'prove' what I've said and done."

One disciple, Matthew, wrote many things about Jesus before recording a single miracle. Matthew didn't have an "ordinary" job like fishing or carpentry—he worked for the first-century IRS. A tax collector aimed to extract from the people everything he could, then turn in only what actually was owed to the government. The emperor didn't care how much his employee took, above the required amount, as long as the emperor got the lion's share.

The Jewish people despised tax collectors, not just for their extortion and corruption but also because they were complicit with the much-hated Romans. But when Matthew met Jesus, everything changed. This loathed man was transformed into a trusted member of Jesus' closest group of followers.

Matthew's gospel, the New Testament's first book, is a major source of miracle stories. But Matthew does not merely document a long list of amazing events. Again, Matthew took his time before even broaching the topic. He vaguely mentions healings in chapter 4, but it isn't until chapter 8 that he finally goes into miracle detail.

We're fully aware that neither Matthew nor any of the other biblical authors divided their writings into chapters and verses. Such demarcations were added much later. But Matthew certainly was intentional about recording many stories about Jesus' life and teachings before he focused on his miracles.

We suspect Matthew had a purpose for delaying this inclusion for later. Apparently he wanted his readers to understand other equally important things about Jesus before the introduction of miracle-working powers. It's obvious he had no intention of portraying Jesus as a magician with a portfolio of tricks.

Matthew wanted us to know that Jesus brought life-giving and life-saving truth. He wanted us to examine Jesus' words before we explored his works. He was saying, in effect, "Seek out and absorb the truth first."

Early on, Matthew says that Jesus went about "teaching . . . proclaiming the good news . . . and healing."[5] Later, with intentionality, he repeats these words in the same order: "teaching . . . proclaiming the good news . . . and healing."[6] Jesus is a teacher, a preacher, and *then* a healer. Matthew seems concerned that we might seek out miracles at the expense of growth and character.

We *should* expect miracles, but they shouldn't be our ultimate goal. While they may be the wind in our sails, we need to keep rowing. Miracles are thrilling, yet they can't compete with the miracle of an authentic life and a focus on always seeking to do the right thing.

EPILOGUE
WHEN MIRACLES DON'T HAPPEN

YOU HOPED AND PRAYED
AND WAITED . . . WHAT NOW?

JIM GARLOW

There's a real possibility you're thinking, *Testimonies about miracles are encouraging. But what about when people pray for miracles and God doesn't answer?* It may be that you, personally, haven't received a miracle you've felt was your only hope.

This question is understandable. It isn't new, either, and the Bible doesn't ignore it. Nor was the Bible itself penned by authors who assumed God always would do as they requested. There are plenty of scriptural examples of people who either did not see their prayer answered right away or did not receive a yes answer at all.

As a pastor, I'm significantly tempted to make this chapter about the various scriptural heroes who had to wait—sometimes wait a very long while—for miracles to happen. And others who, to be frank, never did see the miracle during their lifetime.

Instead, I've chosen to share in a deeply personal way.

We're Still Waiting

Early on I described my wife's battle with cancer and the excruciating journey on which that's led us. When I gladly accepted the invitation to coauthor this book, I was hoping Carol's miracle-healing story would be a rousing start to the first chapter—or perhaps a triumphant conclusion to the last. I was very much praying and trusting that *our* miracle experience could serve to help bolster *your* faith.

Such has not been the case. Our fortieth wedding anniversary cruise had to be delayed because of chemotherapy. It was put off again for unanticipated radiation treatments that required Carol to fly weekly from San Diego to Houston and back, early every Monday morning and late each Thursday night. As Dad, I cleared my schedule so I could manage our home, and I arranged for women to accompany Carol through forty days of treatment.

Her permanent healing has not come. There's no evidence of a miracle—yet.

The aggressive cancer she faces has an incessant recurrence pattern with shorter and shorter remissions. Remissions have, true to form, been telescoped into shorter time spans. Few people survive five years. In fact, I am proofreading this chapter on the fourth anniversary of her original diagnosis. As I've said, for this season of our lives I have a mantra: *"We need a miracle, and we need it now."*

During the rewrite of this very chapter, I was at MD Anderson Cancer Center with my wife. Unfortunately, the radiation oncologist began speaking to us with these sobering words: "I am so sorry; I have very bad news for you."

We'd anticipated we would hear the word *remission*. Instead, the cancer had advanced into Carol's liver. And in my hands was a file with the pages of this chapter—for a book titled *Miracles Are for Real*.

In reality, what we faced was the *absence* of a miracle. But my wife and I are absolutely convinced that the absence of a miracle in no way impugns God's love for us.

I do believe a miracle will come. That's not denial or delusion. That's belief—wholehearted—in a God who performs miracles.

Still, in the distance looms this question: *What if?* What if there's no miracle? What if God doesn't pull through for us when we need him most?

I resolved this issue in 2007, during the late-night and early-morning hours of Thursday, June 21, and Friday, June 22. The euphemistic diagnosis of "there's a mass" had come at 7:09 a.m. on June 20, 2007. Everything—and I mean everything—changed in that moment.

By Friday morning, I'd known we faced this challenge for all of forty-eight hours. It was ripping up my insides. Hunched over my keyboard, I could not stop crying.

The future seemed bleak. I looked to my right, through our foyer, across the music room, and saw the beautiful window treatments Carol had just purchased and arranged to be mounted.

Everything I see reminds me of her, I thought. *If I lose her, how will I possibly survive? Everything in this house, along with most of the things in my life, will remind me of what I will have lost.*

When my tear ducts eventually emptied, I looked back once more at those white wooden blinds, now seemingly the symbol for my potential loss. *"What will I do?"*

At that moment, I found myself saying, "I will not follow the advice of Job's wife!" Her words, found early in the book of Job, are succinct: "Curse God and die!"[1]

That was it. That's the response she believed was most appropriate.

Something rose up from deep within me. A *no* roared from the epicenter of my being: "I will *not* curse God and die. I will *not!*" Continuing on, something more came from within, almost shouting, *"No matter what happens, Lord, I will love you!"*

For me, the matter was resolved; I call this my "knothole moment." I'd been pulled through the knothole of releasing Carol if needed. And it didn't mean I loved her less—quite the opposite. We've fallen more madly in love AD (after disease) than BC (before cancer).

It also didn't mean I would fight for her life any less. In fact, I vaulted into a whirlwind of research, following hundreds of leads that resulted in a three-part "intuitive cancer protocol without scientific evidence" (the phrase used by one of our oncologists). I continue searching to this day.

But it did mean fighting for her life without clenched fists—or certainly not clenched at God. (Again, it's God's enemy—not God—who is to blame for all disease, suffering, heartache, tears, and death.) I could fight for Carol with an "open hand."

Simply put, she's not ultimately mine. She is God's. She was created by him, and she belongs to him. Period.

Of course, I want her. We have been married forty years. I want her for forty more. And that may occur. But I will *not* "curse God and die," in any event. No matter what, I will love my God and remain devoted to him.

Regardless.

Miracle or no miracle, I will press forward. And so can you.

Watching for the Mighty Hand of God

Albert Einstein once said, "There are only two ways to live your life. One is as though nothing is a miracle. The other is as though everything is a miracle."[2] Einstein was known far more for scientific breakthroughs than spiritual insights. But he was on to something here, which brings up another important aspect of what happens when a miracle doesn't occur.

We tend to become so focused on the big thing we're waiting for that we overlook the smaller wonders along the way. We may get so consumed by our pressing need—often justifiably so—that we miss the miracles around us, surrounding us, every day. Most of us are prone to dwelling on what we don't have, and frequently that means we fail to savor and celebrate what we do have.

Kenneth Woodward, in *The Book of Miracles,* writes that there's no word in the Hebrew Bible (almost the entire Old Testament) corresponding to our word *miracle.*[3] This is remarkable, considering how many miracles are recorded there.

How can there be no word for *miracle* in the language that comprises four-fifths of the Bible? Not only would we expect that term to exist, but wouldn't you expect that it would be

247

used over and over? Has something been lost in translation over the passage of several millennia?

Not at all. The answer lies in how the Old Testament writers *do* speak of miracles. They describe amazing, supernatural feats as "mighty works of God." Of course, they also describe ordinary, everyday events as "mighty works of God." That's more than just semantics or linguistic hair-splitting: It powerfully indicates the primary difference between the people of biblical times and the people of today.

We have an immediate mental demarcation between what we can scientifically explain and what we cannot. Some things fit within our plausibility structure—say, a chariot going down from Jerusalem to Jericho—and some don't, such as blind eyes suddenly regaining sight.

"Plausibility structure" refers to the things we think we can take seriously—things that fit neatly within our frame of reference for explainable events. If a trusted mechanic fixed your car and then told you it ran perfectly, that would be plausible to you. If, however, he said he retooled your car so it now flies like a plane, you would say, "I don't think so." That's outside your "plausibility structure"—it's simply not believable.

As "modern" people—those who've lived after the mid-1500s—we tend to divide phenomena into "natural" and "the unexplainable," or "natural" and "supernatural." In the left column we would list things that seem "normal" (explainable); on the right are those that are "abnormal" (unexplainable).

People of faith say the left side is humanly explained, while the right side might be God performing miracles. To skeptics, the "unexplainable" idea is foolishness, so they dismiss anything allegedly done by "God" as superstitious and non-sensical. Everything, they say, can be explained according to the natural order of the universe.

Bona fide agnostics are still a tiny part of the population. The number of atheists is even smaller. Most people—somewhere around 90 percent—are aware of some demarcation point, a type of dividing line between things they understand and things beyond their understanding.

Not so for the ancient Jewish people. In their view of the world, *everything* was done by God. We wouldn't view our daily work as miraculous, but to a Hebrew person the strength to maintain a paying job often was not humanly possible: "Remember the Lord your God, for it is he who gives you the ability to produce wealth."[4] Our ability to make a living is "God's mighty work."

Even something as basic as breathing wasn't perceived merely as a "natural" biological function. It was God himself who originally gave us life: "The Lord God formed a man from the dust of the ground and breathed into his nostrils the breath of life, and the man became a living being."[5]

While some today view conception as the natural, readily explainable, gestational confluence of egg and sperm, the ancients viewed it this way: "You [God] created my inmost being; you knit me together in my mother's womb. I praise you because I am fearfully and wonderfully made; your works are wonderful."[6] Although they understood the human role in producing life, they were equally willing to interpret its creation as the work of God's hand.

There were no natural and supernatural categories. God was held as integrally involved in the daily rising of the sun as in the raising of a person from the dead. *Whether it was an initial creative act or an ongoing work or a singular inter-vention, God was seen at work in all of life.* No aspect was separate from his remarkable action. If all of life is in this sense miraculous, there's no need for a word that highlights *more* majestic and dramatic demonstrations of God's presence and power.

> The heavens are telling the glory of God; they are a marvel-ous display of his craftsmanship. Day and night they keep on telling about God. Without a sound or word, silent in the skies, their message reaches out to all the world. The sun lives in the heavens where God placed it and moves out across the skies as radiant as a bridegroom going to his wedding, or as joyous as an athlete looking forward to a race![7]

We would halfheartedly describe the earth's orbit, gravi-tational pull, and atmospheric conditions. They were *en-thralled*—and, yes, even more thrilled when nature had its normal course interrupted. Notice how Joshua describes a day with twenty-four hours of sunlight:

> The sun stopped in the middle of the sky and delayed going down about a full day. There has never been a day like it before or since, a day when the Lord listened to a human being. Surely the Lord was fighting for Israel![8]

Plainly, not using *miracle* didn't mean the Israelites weren't awed by them. Indeed, these events were so fantastic that they described phenomena in detail, going far beyond a one-word label. God was as much in the explainable as in the miraculous.

Of course you know I'm not suggesting we toss out em-pirical data. I *am* asking you to identify God's remarkable hand behind the "ordinary" aspects of life. In so doing, you might expand your definition of *miraculous*.

All of this, too, brings us back to our response when miracles don't happen—when we pray and hope but nothing apparently is forthcoming. This is painful and troubling, to be sure, and there's no point in denying our feelings. At the same time, we can stop and remember that "God's mighty works" are unfolding in even the smallest details and most mundane events. When we acknowledge and appreciate that all of life is a miracle, we may be reassured and comforted when the one big miracle we're seeking doesn't seem to be happening.

Evidence of God's miracles is all around us, if we'll have eyes to see.

NOTES

Introduction: A Miracle at Any Moment

1. C. S. Lewis, from an essay called "Miracles," originally preached as a sermon in St. Jude on the Hill Church in London, November 26, 1942. Walter Hooper, who edited Lewis's literary estate, placed "Miracles" in the book *God in the Dock* (Grand Rapids, MI: Eerdmans, 1994).

2. Ephesians 3:20

Chapter 1: Do Miracles Still Happen?

1. Statistics from *USA Today*/Gallup poll and the Pew Forum on Religion. For more detail, visit: www.washingtonpost.com/wp-dyn/content/story/2008/06/23/ST2008062300818.html and www.gallup.com/poll/27682/onethird-americans-believe-bible-literally-true.asp.

2. See Matthew 8:29–32.

Chapter 4: The Meaning of Miracles

1. David Weddle, *Miracles: Wonder and Meaning in World Religions* (New York: New York University Press, 2010), xii-xiii.

2. "Miracles" in *The Encyclopedia of Judaism,* ed. Geoffrey Wigoder (New York: Macmillan General Reference, 1989), 493.

3. John Wimber wrote and lectured extensively on "Healings, Signs and Wonders."

Chapter 5: What Skeptics Say

1. In our previous book, *Encountering Heaven and the Afterlife* (Minneapolis: Bethany House, 2010), we told many stories with the same dramatically life-changing effect.

2. www.randi.org/site/index.php/1m-challenge.html

3. The originally pledged amount of $100 (in 1968) has been increased by 10,000 percent over the decades.

4. www.randi.org/jr/200510/102105herbs.html#11 (in *Swift,* 21 October 2005, "Good Intentions").

5. Caspar McCloud, *Nothing Is Impossible* (Gainsville, GA: Praxis Press, 2006).

6. *The Bob Siegel Show,* May 11, 2006, KCBQ 1170, San Diego.

7. According to a 2005 survey, 76 percent of doctors said they believe in God and 59 percent in an afterlife; 55 percent said their religious beliefs influenced how they practice medicine (*Associated Press,* 06/23/05).

8. "Of Miracles," 115–116, as quoted by Dan Barker, *Did Jesus Really Rise from the Dead?* This article originally appeared in *Abuse Your Illusions: The Disinformation Guide to Media Mirages and Establishment Lies,* ed. Russ Kick (New York: The Disinformation Company, 2003).

9. That is, pseudopigraphical.

10. Robert J. Miller, ed., *The Complete Gospels: Annotated Scholars Version* (Sonoma, CA: Polebridge, 1992), 363–372.

11. See Luke 3:23.

12. Acts 4:6–7

13. Acts 4:14

14. http://www.skepdic.com/miracles.html

15. Richard Dawkins, *The God Delusion* (New York: Mariner, 2008), 14.

16. Norman L. Geisler and Frank Turek, *I Don't Have Enough Faith to Be an Atheist* (Wheaton, IL: Crossway, 2004).

17. C. S. Lewis, *Miracles* (New York: Simon & Schuster, 1996), 65.

18. See "Stand to Reason" at www.str.org. "There's no wishful thinking here. No leap of faith. No blind faith. Just a reasonable step of trust—trusting something we have good reason to believe is true" (www.str.org/site/News2?page =NewsArticle&id=8817).

Chapter 6: "God, Are You Listening?"

1. See Matthew 8:1–4.

2. See Matthew 8:5–13.

3. See Matthew 8:14–15.

Chapter 7: Wonder-Workers and Miracle Makers

1. One expansive list, found at www.christiananswers.net/dictionary/miracle .html, claims there are at least 120 biblical miracles. The apologist Henry Morris, for one, contends there are many more.

2. Kenneth Woodward, *The Book of Miracles* (New York: Simon & Schuster, 2000), 36.

3. John 5:19–20

4. Acts 9:32–33

5. Acts 16:26

6. Regarding Irenaeus, see www.pneumafoundation.org/resources/articles/irenaeus-dvreeland.pdf and www.gnosis.org/library/advh1.htm.

7. See *Thy Kingdom Come: A Blumhardt Reader,* ed. Vernard Eller (Farmington, PA: Plough, 2007), 19.

8. http://en.wikipedia.org/wiki/Johann_Blumhardt

9. Some historians attribute to Wigglesworth more than twenty miracles involving people raised from the dead.

10. Dennis Lindsay is featured in chapter 16.

11. See 1 Corinthians 12:9–10.

Chapter 8: God's Favor or Good Fortune?

1. Quotations from www.msnbc.msn.com/id/21134540/vp/42098348#42098348

2. See John 10:10.

3. See chapter 2.

Chapter 9: Powerful Promptings

1. Acts 9:4–6

2. See verse 11.

3. Acts 9:11

4. Acts 9:13–14

5. Acts 9:15

6. See Acts 9:18–19.

7. 1 Corinthians 12:8 (NASB)

8. 1 Corinthians 12:8 (NLT); see 1 Corinthians 12:7–11 for context.

9. See John 5:19.

10. See John 5:30.

11. See Joshua 7:10–11.

12. In John 4:16–18; see John 4:4–42 for context.

13. See 2 Kings 5.

14. For more on this topic, see our book *Heaven and the Afterlife* (Minneapolis: Bethany House, 2009).

Chapter 10: The Dancing Hand of God

1. On this approach, see www.templeprayer.com.

2. See 1 Corinthians 12:7. Specifically, here, the manifestation of the Spirit's gifts to believers, among which are gifts of healing and miraculous powers.

3. See www.thesecret.tv/living.html.

4. See James L. Garlow and Rick Marschall, *The Secret Revealed* (Nashville: FaithWords, 2007).

5. Rhonda Byrne, *The Power* (New York: Atria, 2006).

Chapter 11: Back From the Dead

1. A June 6, 1983, account in the Fort Worth *Star-Telegram* refers to this incident as a "stroke," though Jesse McElreath is adamant the individuals present were sure Milton Green had no pulse for an extended period of time.

2. See other details at www.wikipedia.org/wiki/Smith_Wigglesworth#Healing.

3. Albert J. Hebert, *Saints Who Raised the Dead: True Stories of 400 Resurrection Miracles* (Charlotte: Tan Books, 2004; rev. ed.); originally titled *Raised From the Dead.*

4. See 2 Kings 4:8–36.

5. See Luke 8:49–56.

6. See John 11.

7. Cf. 1 John 3:2.

8. Having addressed this topic at greater length in two previous books—*Heaven and the Afterlife* (Minneapolis: Bethany House, 2009) and *Encountering Heaven and the Afterlife* (Minneapolis: Bethany House, 2010)—we're touching on it just briefly here.

9. See John 20:26–29.

10. See 1 Corinthians 15:45; see also Romans 5.

11. John 11:25–26.

12. See John 11:17–44.

13. Many thanks to CBN and Sheryl Fountain, whose story "Jeff Markin: Back From the Dead, Reborn Into the Light" first appeared on the Christian Broadcasting Network's *700 Club* program on September 15, 2010. This feature provided much of the information in the retelling here. See www.cbn.com/700club/features/amazing/Jeff-Markin-Chauncey-Crandall-091510.aspx. For a more detailed account of this event, see Dr. Chauncey Crandall's book *Raising the Dead: A Doctor Encounters the Miraculous* (Faith Words, 2010). Also visit Dr. Crandall's website at www.chaunceycrandall.com.

Chapter 12: Heaven's Special Forces

1. This story originally appeared in James L. Garlow and Keith Wall, *Encountering Heaven and the Afterlife: True Stories From People Who Have Glimpsed the World Beyond* (Minneapolis: Bethany House Publishers, 2010), 89–95.

2. For a full retelling of these and other accounts, please see *Encountering Heaven and the Afterlife.*

3. See Joshua 5:13–15.

4. See Daniel 10:4–9.

5. See Daniel 10:10ff.

6. See Luke 1–2.

7. See 1 Peter 1:12.

8. See Hebrews 1:14.

9. See Hebrews 2:7–8.

10. Some scholars interpret the angelic equation in Revelation 5:11 literally, while others treat it figuratively.

Chapter 13: Miracle Mongers: Phonies and Frauds

1. *Leap of Faith,* Paramount Pictures, 1992. Written by Janus Cercone. Directed by Richard Pearce.

2. Sinclair Lewis, *Elmer Gantry* (New York: Harcourt, 1927).

3. See THE WORD on The Word of Faith (a GroupBlog), "Marjoe Gortner: Proof That Some Christians Will Fall for Anything" (accessed 5/24/11) at: http://webcache.googleusercontent.com/search?q=cache:aBsxU7mqkTAJ:thewordon thewordoffaithinfoblog.com/2009/05/26/marjoe-gortner/+marjoe+gortner&cd =11&hl=en&ct=clnk&gl=us&source=www.google.com.

4. *Marjoe,* produced and directed by Howard Smith and Sarah Kamochan, won the 1972 Academy Award for Best Documentary Feature.

5. Matthew 7:15, 21–23

6. Joe Nickell, *Looking for a Miracle* (New York: Prometheus, 1999), 137–141.

7. James Randi, *The Faith Healers* (New York: Prometheus, 1989), 2, 147.

8. See the article "Peter Popoff, Holy Water, and Financial Seeds Network" at http://endtimespropheticwords.wordpress.com.

9. On Peter Popoff, see the following additional sources: William Packard, *Evangelism in America: From Tents to TV* (iUniverse, 2000); Carl Leon Bankston, *Great Events From History: Modern Scandals 1904–2008* (Pasadena, CA: Salem, 2009); "Selling Salvation?" ABC News report, May 11, 2007.

10. We mentioned Wimber in chapter 4 and spoke of his methodology in chapter 7.

Chapter 14: What's Old Is New

1. See 1 Kings 18.

2. Bert Ghezzi, *Mystics and Miracles* (Chicago: Loyola, 2002), 155–160.

3. As quoted by Carol Neiman, *The Extraordinary, the Impossible, and the Divine* (New York: Viking Penguin, 1995), 90.

4. See Luke 24; Acts 1.

5. See Acts 8.

6. In Neiman, *The Extraordinary, the Impossible, and the Divine,* 89.

Chapter 15: In the Nick of Time

1. John 11:21

2. The Genesis 22 account of Abraham's near-sacrifice of Isaac contains one of the most important truths in the entire Bible. Regrettably, we cannot go into detail on this here, but for an extensive explanation of the event's theological significance, see James L. Garlow, *The Covenant* (Kansas City: Beacon Hill, 1999).

3. See Psalm 46:1.

4. See Genesis 37–50.

5. The apostle Paul, in Romans 5:12–21, magnificently explains this reality in the context of sin and salvation.

6. See Revelation 21–22.

7. Proverbs 3:5

Chapter 16: Are Some People "Miracle Magnets"?

1. See chapter 10, "The Dancing Hand of God."

2. We all desire to be more effective in prayer, and to see prayer work effectively. For much more about the workings of prayer and the authority God grants believers, see James L. Garlow, *The Covenant* (2nd ed., 2003), chapters 2–5, 8–10.

3. Citing Mark 11:22

4. *God Still Heals: Answers to Your Questions About Divine Healing*, by James L. Garlow and Carol Jane Garlow (Indianapolis: Wesleyan, 2005), identifies eighteen different *potential* causative factors in the blockage of healing. See especially pages 251–252.

5. Arthur Pierson, quoted at www.internetmonk.com/archive/quotes.

6. Gloria Copeland, Kenneth Copeland's wife, has said, "The true evidence of prosperity is a holy life."

7. We certainly do not suggest that there's something inherently sinful or wrong in the moments of doubt that are normal to all human experience. As we've shown elsewhere, miracles ultimately aren't founded on human faith but on God's love (which doesn't discount our faith but rather contextualizes it). Knowing this can bring profound comfort to us all—whether or not we're "faith giants."

Chapter 17: Beware of Being a Miracle Chaser

1. This story was brought to our attention by Howie Shute, missionary with the Church of the Nazarene, Africa Region. Shute corroborates this account, as do many others. (See also Daniel 3.)

2. See John 20:30–31.

3. See John 4:48.

4. See John 20:29.

5. See Matthew 4:23–25.

6. See Matthew 9:35–38.

Epilogue: When Miracles Don't Happen

1. Job 2:9

2. *The Expanded Quotable Einstein*, ed. Alice Calaprice (Princeton, NJ: Princeton University Press, 2000), 319.

3. Kenneth Woodward, *The Book of Miracles* (New York: Simon & Schuster, 2000), 34.

4. Deuteronomy 8:18

5. Genesis 2:7

6. Psalm 139:13–14

7. Psalm 19:1–5 TLB

8. Joshua 10:13–14

ACKNOWLEDGMENTS

FROM JIM GARLOW:
All books involve the work of so many more than those whose names appear on the cover. This one is no exception.

I write this page not out of perfunctory obligation but from a heart overflowing with gratitude. I cannot adequately express what each of these has done for me. It's no overstatement to say that, without them, there would have been no book.

Keith Wall, Coauthor

Keith Wall has been absolutely wonderful throughout this process, carrying an enormous portion of our shared load, handling a rash of deadlines, and taking elongated phone calls, all with grace and in stride. We've been privileged to write several books separately before partnering on this one. Our third together (may there be more!) was written under great stress and pressure (unrelated to the writing itself). This season in both our lives has been one of intense testing, yet God has seen us through it all. Thank you, thank you, Keith. You consistently demonstrate the life of Christ within, and you're the epitome of a Christian gentleman.

Bob Siegel, Writing & Research

I give special recognition to Bob Siegel, who assisted with so much right up to the final deadline. Bob is an exceptional apologist, thinker, debater, radio host, and writer. Considering the amount of advice and input he gave, along with research and original writing on some of the most difficult chapters, I fully expect him soon to be writing more books. Thank you, Bob.

Jeff Dunn, Writing & Research

Jeff Dunn has been one of my best "book" friends, seeing me through so many projects over the years. In the past he's played many roles: acquisitions editor, literary agent, general advisor, and, for lack of a better title, author-counselor. He likewise did some writing, and at great sacrifice to his own schedule. His view is, "If you need help, I'll do anything to help you" . . . and he did! Thank you, Jeff, for your infectious spirit for life and for the portions of this book you helped me write under challenging deadlines.

Kyle Duncan, Acquisitions Editor

Kyle Duncan, the man who first conceived of this book (and the previous two books Keith and I co-wrote), was and is our finest cheerleader-advisor and—when we've needed it, and in all the right ways—our confronter, on all three books.

Thank you, Kyle, for what you do and who you are. You're a man of high integrity.

Christopher Soderstrom, Content Editor

Editors, I believe, have one of the most difficult tasks: informing occasionally insecure and defensive authors that they need to cut (among other things) many pages. In addition, they have to challenge entire paragraphs at a time. This is my twelfth book, and by now I've learned that they're usually (always?) right. Thank you, Christopher, for having what it takes to stretch us, challenge us, and question us when needed, even when "it ain't fun!"

Bethany House Publishers

In addition to Kyle and Christopher, the entire team of employees at Bethany House, part of the Baker Publishing Group, is such a joy to work with, year after year. Author/publisher relationships can be strained. Bethany House has strived to work through details in a way that has blessed this author and honored the name of Jesus. Thank you, BHP, for the privilege of partnering with you.

Tracy Burger, Administrative Assistant

I praise God every day for Tracy Burger, who manages thousands of details without becoming flustered . . . *and* functions drama free. Tracy, you make a very hard task appear so easy. I don't believe in cloning, but if I did, I'd clone you—you are remarkable!

Pam Dahl, Assistant

Thank you to the steady, unflappable Pam Dahl, who helped manage some of this book's critical logistics. She's always there, with a *classic* servant's heart. Thank you so much, Pam.

Skyline Wesleyan Church

To our pastors, support staff, board, and congregation in Rancho San Diego, California: Thank you for tolerating full sermons and short illustrations on miracles that allowed me to process as I wrote. Without knowing it, you were my captive sounding board. I thank God daily for the privilege of sharing in your journeys with Christ.

Family

To my wife, my children, and my extended family: Thank you for your patience during the seemingly endless months when I disappeared to write. Even though they've decided to engrave on my tombstone "At least he's not at his computer," with this work's completion I'll now attempt to reemerge and make up for some of the time I have been consumed by this project.

Others (only a few of whom can be named)

Special thanks to the Rancho San Diego Library, which allowed me to check out books well beyond (or so I suspect) the standard length of time. Your patience was a blessing to me. Thank you.

Much gratitude to Joanne Getter, who worked on details so quietly, behind the scenes, that I never found out until after the manuscript was completed. Thank you, Joanne.

I am so grateful for all those who submitted stories, even if, regrettably, your stories don't appear on these pages. Without you, there would have been no book. Thank you for entrusting your stories to us. You've blessed so many by sharing your lives.

FROM KEITH WALL:
Plenty of writers complain about the endless hours of toil in isolation and seclusion. I am exceedingly blessed to have a loyal band of friends who urge me on with wisdom, understanding, and healthy doses of laughter. Heartfelt and heaping thanks to:

Alan Wartes, who contributed significantly to this book and has contributed even more significantly to my life;

Kyle Duncan, more than a publisher and more than a friend, a soul-mate brother;

Dave Kopp, writer and editor extraordinaire, who's talked me down from more than a few ledges, always with grace and compassion;

Karen Linamen, my longtime pal and sometime collaborator, whose enthusiasm and optimism are equal only to her creative genius;

Greg Carter, whose unfailingly positive attitude lifts my spirits and bolsters my faith.

I am grateful, too, for the highly skilled (and long-suffering) team at Bethany House—Dave Horton, Julie Smith, Tim Peterson, Brett Benson, and so many others. A big round of applause for our editor, Christopher Soderstrom, who guided us with extraordinary patience and deftness. In the process, he has become a good friend.

Jim Garlow and I began our writing partnership four years ago as an "arranged marriage," brought together by our mutual friend Kyle Duncan. In the intervening years, that professional relationship has deepened into genuine love, respect, and admiration. Amid daunting crises and challenges, Jim has persevered with utmost integrity and grace.

I'm extremely grateful to my family—Robin, Juliana, and Logan—for patiently enduring life with a creative type. Not always a smooth ride. But what an adventure! Thanks for sharing it with me.

ABOUT THE AUTHORS

JAMES L. GARLOW is senior pastor of Skyline Church in San Diego, chairman of Renewing American Leadership, and a nationwide speaker and author of several books, including *Cracking Da Vinci's Code,* with a half million in print. He has appeared on CNN, FOX, NBC, and other media outlets. *The Garlow Perspective* commentary is heard on over 800 radio outlets. He has Master's degrees from Princeton and Asbury seminaries and a PhD from Drew University. Jim and his family live in San Diego, California.

KEITH WALL, a twenty-five-year publishing veteran, has been an award-winning magazine editor, radio scriptwriter, and online columnist. He currently writes full time in collaboration with numerous bestselling authors. He and his family live in Colorado Springs.

Get to know Dr. Jim Garlow...

www.JimGarlow.com (Personal)

www.SkylineChurch.org (Pastoral)

www.ToRenewAmerica.org (National)

Connect on Facebook

Hear Dr. Jim Garlow on his radio commentary
The Garlow Perspective.

(For station listings, go to www.AmbassadorAdvertising.com)